True Rebellion

VOLUME 3
Finding the Rebel Within

Finding the Rebel Within

Copyright © 2026 by Vishrant. All rights reserved.

No part of this book may be reproduced, stored in a retrieval system, or transmitted in any form or by any means, including electronic, mechanical, photocopying, recording, or otherwise, or translated into any language, without prior written permission from the author and publisher, except for brief quotations used in reviews or articles.

True Rebellion Vol. 3
Finding the Rebel Within
ISBN:
978-1-7638511-4-6 - ebook
978-1-7638511-5-3 - paperback
The Vishrant Buddhist Society

Disclaimer

This book is intended for educational and informational purposes only. The insights and teachings shared within this book reflect the personal experiences and understandings of Vishrant and are not intended as professional advice. The content of this book should not be used as a substitute for medical, psychological, legal, or financial advice. Readers are encouraged to use their discernment and seek professional guidance where necessary.

The author and publisher make no representations or warranties regarding the completeness, accuracy, or applicability of the teachings presented. The journey of self-inquiry and spiritual awakening is deeply personal, and each individual is responsible for their own path and experiences.

Contents

Overview 5
Introduction 7

CHAPTER ONE
How Do You Prepare The Mind For Enlightenment? 11

CHAPTER TWO
The Call to Enlightenment 35

CHAPTER THREE
How Do I Get Free of Suffering? 63

CHAPTER FOUR
What is it like to live as Awareness? 87

CHAPTER FIVE
The Price for Enlightenment 113

CHAPTER SIX
The Light of Awareness 139

CHAPTER SEVEN
What is Required to Wake Up 163

CHAPTER EIGHT
From Darkness to Light 187

CHAPTER NINE
Going with the Flow 211

CHAPTER TEN
Why Taking Offence Doesn't Work 235

About Vishrant 259

Overview

True Rebellion is a four-part series delving deeply into the most crucial challenges faced by today's seekers. Vishrant's teachings are focused on seekers living and working in the marketplace, just as he did in his years-long journey towards Enlightenment.

Each volume of the True Rebellion series provides critical insight into the private workings of Vishrant's Mystic Heart Mystery School located in the hills of Perth near the historic Araluen Estate. Seekers from around the world attend in person and online in what may be the only Mystery School personally run by an enlightened master. Vishrant credits his years in Osho's Mystery School in Oregon and Pune for his own preparation for Enlightenment.

Vishrant sees that teachers who claim "there is nothing to do" are selling seekers short. He says seekers deserve the truth full strength and to understand that the obstacles that are in the way of Enlightenment must be undone if the seeker is to reach the ultimate. Although those who seek awakening must ultimately surrender themselves in the achievement, Vishrant's teachings are focused on helping ardent students of higher consciousness ready themselves for that awakening to occur.

The True Rebellion series was produced with this expressed purpose in mind: to highlight and deeply examine the key challenges and obstacles seekers face as hindrances to Enlightenment. The four-book series explores topics including family and work commitments, self-doubt, failure patterns, inherited programming, and the role of the mind and the need for scepticism, openness, present-moment awareness and trust on the path to higher consciousness and Enlightenment.

Vishrant's dialogues with students also provide numerous real-world examples from the master's own journey towards Enlightenment after he found himself as Truth in 1999 following many years of totality as a seeker. The exchanges recorded in the True Rebellion series contain Vishrant's trademark wit and humour, as well as the cutting insights and ruthless honesty he says every seeker must also develop for themselves.

Introduction

About 34 years ago, I had this realisation that I had wasted 33 years of my life in service of myself and in service of being successful in the material world. And I'm not saying there's anything wrong with that, but for me, it cost me my Heart.

As a businessman, I'd turned myself into a war machine and I was pretty good at it, but 34 years ago, I had an awakening of the Heart and it changed my life completely. I could not see any point in making money for the sake of making money anymore. I felt that it was repetitious, and for me, it was relatively easy.

So after having this awakening, which disappeared, I realised there was something very, very valuable here for human beings, and that was the Heart or unconditional love. It didn't take too long, from that point. It took about nine months before I walked into my companies and gave them to my staff as a gift. I cared about my staff. They'd been with me for 10 years or more and I didn't want to see the company sold and them possibly get sacked or whatever could have happened to them, so I gave my staff everything, including the office furniture. So 35 of them were reasonably happy and I walked out broke.

I had realised that as long as I was in business as a publisher, which is a very hectic business, I was too closed, too defended, too protected to perceive love. I had come to an understanding that love was possible for human beings – unconditional love – but only under certain conditions. And those conditions were openness, vulnerability and being undefended.

So we hear about people wearing their hearts on their sleeves. Well, yes, you have to be that open – and the problem with that, of course, is that if you are that open, the world will hurt you. The world is pretty rough. People betray you. They let you down. They say things. They steal. All sorts of things happen that don't go the way you would like and quite often we close to defend ourselves. In so doing, we cut ourselves off from the perception of love and love is really the true jewel of consciousness.

After about four years of wandering around Australia, barefoot, as a bum, I found my Heart. Existence broke me. I surrendered enough of my defence systems – enough of my resistance to life – to perceive love regularly. I had developed a pattern of undoing defence systems and being open, and as time went by, more and more love was perceived.

It's kind of like around that point that I realised there's nothing else worth doing here. I could never really find a true purpose for life or a meaningful life, even though I had been looking since I was a young teenager. But if I'm going to be here, what I decided was, I might as well love. And when love affects the mind, you just want to take care of everything and everyone. That's how beautiful it is. The good, the bad, and the ugly. Your enemies and your friends. Love is most magnificent, but there's a price for it. It is your openness. It is your undefendedness. It is your non-resistance to life and your acceptance of life as it is.

And that, for a lot of us, especially for me, was very difficult. I had gone to a private school where I was taught how to win at any cost and I took that into my 20s, into business as a war machine. I had to dismantle the war machine. I had to take down all of its defence systems. I had to start to walk through the world open, even while being attacked, because I felt that love was more important than anything. I'm not really talking about personal love here. Not "I love you" or "I love my partner" or "I love my children". I love everybody and everything. And this is possible if you're willing to be open, if you're willing to experience the discomfort of being open, because it is uncomfortable to be open, to be around the roughness of the world we live in. It is hard and it takes courage.

So people get into higher consciousness and they start looking for Enlightenment. But while you're looking, you've still got to be here, and as far as I'm concerned, the only way to be here that's worthwhile is the Way of the Heart. This path is the path of non-resistance. People say "Well, if I'm non-resistant, I'll be ineffective in the world; if I'm open, I'll be ineffective in the world". Not true. We can do everything from openness. We just think we can't. We can be very effective, but from a place that will support Heart rather than from a place that just supports survival.

So sometimes I talk about Enlightenment, but towards Enlightenment there's a way to live in this place, a beautiful way to live in this place, and this is the Way of the Heart. It's up to you as to whether you do or you don't. No one will ever make you. No one will ever make you take your defences down. You have to voluntarily do it yourself, and I'd never ever tell anyone that it was easy because it's not. Changing any default pattern in the mind is difficult. It takes a fair bit of practice over a fair bit of time, but what else you got to do? How beautiful is your life? Because when you serve Heart, it may be uncomfortable, but it's beautiful.

CHAPTER ONE

How Do You Prepare The Mind For Enlightenment?

V: *dialog from Vishrant*
S: *dialog from student*
~ *separate dialogues from different speakers*

S: Hello Vishrant, can you please talk about how to prepare the mind for Enlightenment?
V: In some spiritual circles, there's this belief that you can go directly to Enlightenment and that awareness can become aware of itself and stay aware of itself simply through self-inquiry or some other accident, but in my experience, that's just not true. The mind has to be prepared to support what is actually found, so if it can't support what's found, more than likely, awareness or consciousness will go back to the mind and the person will start living as ego-based reality again, rather than being-based reality.

In being-based reality, you're living as Beingness and nothing touches. In ego-based reality, you're identified as an "I" and everything touches. The ego, which is the part of the mind that is identified with the body and the mind as itself, has to learn to be accepting, has to learn to be quiet, because as long as it's creating noise, as long as it's creating resistance, it will attract awareness back to itself.

People can go into self-inquiry Advaita Vedanta-style, self-inquire, find themselves as Truth and then come out into the material world again and lose it pretty rapidly – not that it can be lost as it's always there, but awareness shifts away from itself back onto the mind and a person finds themselves basically as a person again, ego-based, because the mind has not really supported what it has found. This has created contractions. It has attracted awareness back to itself.

A mind that can accept life as it is is a mind that will support Enlightenment. In Buddhism, we call this an equanimous mind, a mind that stays level. Even when being attacked, it doesn't react. It might respond, but it doesn't react with contraction. And so the mind, it plays a part in a big way, in supporting Enlightenment. It is the mind that practises meditation, it is the mind that practises self-inquiry, it is the mind that practises openness, it is the mind that will support Heart, it is the mind that will support the work healing the wounds of the Heart, and it is the mind that will support Enlightenment. It develops a love affair with Truth. It develops a love affair with the Heart. The mind itself becomes a servant of Truth, a servant of Heart, and in that service, it lays itself down in unconditional surrender. And it is in unconditional surrender that Enlightenment can stay.

If it's not staying, if it's flip-flopping, it's just satoris. Experience of Truth itself, back to ego-based reality, experience of Truth itself back to ego-based reality, a flip-flopping affair or half-baked Enlightenment, if you like. Full Enlightenment is when awareness stays on itself 24 hours a day, seven days a week, and doesn't leave itself. Then the person is no longer living as a person. Truth is living, aware of itself, fully aware of itself. And the person disappears because it's seen for what it is: not real.

The ego thinks it's real because it has a past and it projects to the future and it analyses. But you take away all of your imagination and the future projections imagined – the past is imagined – take away all dream and what is actually here? The only thing that's left here is pure awareness. Yet we miss that, because it doesn't move and it doesn't make noise. It's absolutely still and silent. But it is always here. Most of the time, human beings live as an ego that thinks it's been somewhere and thinks it's going somewhere, identified with a body, identified with the mind, identified with a life and a projection to the future. This is simply not true. Without imagination, this can't exist.

You try looking for the "I" sometime. You won't find it. It's not there. It's imagined. But who we really are, that that is aware of the mind, that that is aware of the "I", now that's interesting, because that's who we really are. Now, holding that as a memory is not good enough. For Enlightenment, awareness has to stay aware of itself. Memory is simply another dream. It's not Enlightenment. The mind can support this by getting out of the way. Gautama the Buddha sat under a Bodhi tree and surrendered and awakening occurred. People quite often don't understand what surrender is. It's the mind that is surrendered and that means the mind is flat-lined. It's not moving. It's a death. It's a death. It's gone. It's flat-lined. And in this non-interference, this non-controlling space, awareness can stay aware of itself. So all spiritual teachers endeavour to help people wake up, but work on the mind is imperative.

Learning to not react, learning to be okay with life as it is, learning to be present to reality instead of present to dream – these are things that the mind can do to support higher consciousness and support Enlightenment. And that's going to be up to you because nobody can do it for you.

Are there any questions, any statements or any challenges to this teaching today?
S: When dancing or listening to music, I'll have emotional expressions and thinking. So how are we supposed to maintain a witness? Because once I maintain a witness, the emotions stop.
V: Yes. Yes, in maintaining a witness, we become detached from the mind and we don't get caught in its drama anymore. The drama might still be going, the story might be still going, but because of detachment, we're no longer caught in it. We're no longer locked in. We're just witnessing it. This is really nice because in this, we don't suffer, and in this, we get to see that we are not the mind and we never were, we're the witness of it. Whether you're dancing or you're just sitting, it doesn't make any difference. Just witness what's happening. Become the witness. Just watch.

~

S: How would I know if I'm ready for awakening?
V: You won't. You won't. It's ultimately an accident. You can self-inquire and possibly turn awareness back on itself, but whether it stays there or it doesn't stay there, man, you don't know, you don't. It's an accident, it happens. Or it doesn't happen. All you can do from the perspective of being ego-based is prepare the ground, a little bit like a farmer prepares the ground for a seed. Puts the seed in, supplies maybe fertiliser and water, but whether the seed takes or not? Well, that's up to a whole pile of other things. It's in a way like an accident. All you can do, the best you can do is prepare the ground. Get the mind ready to support what's going to be found or what is found.

~

S: So is self-inquiry just a means to turn awareness back to itself?
V: Yes. That's correct.

~

S: What is the biggest obstacle for the mind's higher consciousness and Enlightenment?
V: It's resistance to life. It's constant "no". It's constant desiring things to be different than how they are and putting resistance into them. Resistance is the biggest obstacle because it locks awareness onto the mind. Stop resisting life. Accept life as it is and get free. Every time we resist life, every time we desire and put resistance into that desire, we create dissatisfaction for ourselves. We create suffering for ourselves. We don't need to. Accept life as it is and stop suffering or continue to resist aggressively and suffer. You are in

charge because you're creating your thoughts. You're creating the resistance. It's up to you.

~

S: Dear Vishrant, I love you. About one year ago, while listening for the first time to our spiritual teacher, I felt his words open my chest and started pouring love inside. For the next two months, everything was wonderful. But after that, all of a sudden, while listening to one of his guided meditations, a very big pain occurred around the heart and soon after other intense symptoms followed: very high heartbeats, heart pain, and a sensation that behind my chest something is moving, like a wave. Also, there is a fear that I might get sick or die. I did medical tests and they are all good for the time being. On the other hand, I feel that my relationships improved a lot and I've started to experience glimpses of unconditional love. What do you advise regarding the physical pain and symptoms, because they worry me, with immense gratitude for your answer?

V: Whether they're physical or they're energetic, acceptance is always the beginning. You always accept what is. You always begin with acceptance. Now, if you've been playing with awakened teachers and you've been in that energy field, well, there's going to be an opening because the energy field that's carried by someone who's awake expands everything. It opens it. It opens doors that have been closed for years. It takes away coping mechanisms. Now that can be very beautiful, because you can have an experience of Heart, but at the same time, you've got to remember that most human adults have quite a lot of repressed emotionality, so when you get opened up and your coping mechanisms get undone, that pain can come out. The pain coming out is something that you've repressed that is finally leaving. If the doctors say there's nothing wrong with your heart, and you've had that physical examination, then I would suspect that it's energetic wounding that is actually leaving because of the openings that you've had in meditations in contact with someone who's awake. Just make it okay. It's an old friend, finally leaving. Okay.

~

S: Recently my desire for so much seems to be dissipating. Every time I start a new business or reach out for something that previously would make me happy, I see it's another way of escaping and it feels pointless. So now, I just sit with this emptiness. It's not depression, but literally empty. Not good or bad. I have no energy to do anything except meditate and listen to satsangs with you or recorded teachings from masters. I'm worried I'll not be able to survive in the world anymore. I'd be very grateful if you can comment on this or have any advice for me? Is this just a phase?

V: From my perspective, the only thing that is worthwhile doing here is to wake up, to actually finally come home and live as your true nature. Now if that's what's happening to you, give it your totality. Hold nothing back because it is in this totality that people wake up and stay awake. I'll leave you with that.

~

S: Hey Vishrant, can I get your blessings for my meditation practice and hopefully come and hang out with you someday?

V: I love everyone. If you call that a blessing, well, it's a blessing, but I don't really give blessings. I just love everybody. That'll do, and if you want to come and hang out, you can. I'm here for seekers.

~

S: I feel like a zombie listening to music because once I witness, I stop my emotions led by the music. Is it supposed to feel emotionless?

V: Thoughts come and go like clouds in the sky come and go. Emotions –which are similar to thoughts – come and go, like clouds in the sky. My interest is the sky. What doesn't come and go? What is always here? What is the background that everything is appearing in? Who are you really?

~

S: Where do you draw the line between helping others and accepting all of the violence and unkindness that exists in the world? In other words, how much do you try to help lessen the horrendous things that happen in the world and how much do you accept that people hurt other people, animals, and the environment and that's the way it is? Thank you for all that you do.

V: I accept everything as it is. Why would I not? It's the way it is. The moment we don't accept life as it is we create suffering for ourselves and we bring more darkness onto this planet. The way the world is is the way the world is. I don't see mistakes really. I just see karma playing out. You can get caught in right, wrong, good and bad and suffer incredibly because of the resistance you offer inside those things. Or you can just accept life as it is and light up as many people as you can. What can you do to lift others? What can you do to make others feel a little better? This world is in a lot of ways tragic. There's a lot of suffering. People hide it. There's a lot of suffering. What can you do to bring a little bit more light into this place? You definitely don't bring light into this place by going into contraction and resistance. Practise acceptance and your consciousness levels will rise. Practise resistance and your consciousness levels will sink. It's your choice.

~

S: I've been vulnerable lately and I have started being more expressive to my parents, which is new. I even hug my mum daily which is also new. Vishrant, is this openness?

V: Openness is allowing the world to pass through you, offering no resistance whatsoever. In this openness, you are totally, absolutely vulnerable. There is nothing in the way anymore. And this openness, in this level of openness, there is no "I" because even that is a form of resistance. Openness is a pathway to Enlightenment. From my perspective, openness counts for everything. Hugging your mother has probably got some openness in it. How about being open with everybody? And I'm not suggesting hugging – people might get offended – but how about being open with everybody all of the time? Walking this world vulnerable, walking this world in a way that supports heart and love? This is the Way of the Heart. This is the Beauty Way. This is also the bhakti path towards Enlightenment. Heck, yeah, go for it. Good to talk to you.

~

S: If Enlightenment has nothing to do with the mind, why does the mind need to be prepared?

V: It seems that awareness that's aware of the mind is locked onto the mind like a magnet. It's not aware of itself in human beings or animals. It has no awareness of itself in human beings and animals. It's locked onto the mind in humans, but because humans are intelligent, they have the ability to turn awareness back to itself and they can do that through self-inquiry and through meditation. It's a possibility. That's one thing. Having awareness stay on itself, that's a completely other story. If you've got a mind that is constantly attracting awareness back to itself, well, that's not going to work very well at all. If you've got a mind that is really quite calm, awareness can quite easily stay on itself. It's up to you. You produce the way you think. It is true, the mind doesn't have anything to do with Beingness really, awareness really, awareness is just aware of it. But in my experience, for awareness to stay on awareness, particularly in the early stages, the mind needs to be quiet. The mind needs to be relaxed, needs to be at ease. It needs to be equanimous. But check it out, find out for yourself, don't take my word for anything, ever. Just look where I'm pointing.

~

S: How can one break the identification with thoughts and emotions and just watch them?

V: Okay, so there's a bit of a fallacy there. The only way that identification can be broken with the mind is for someone to wake up and be awake. That's the only way because then it's clear that you're not the mind. It's clear you are not that, so the identification can't be there. Becoming the witness, witnessing the mind, identification can drop, but that's not that permanent. It is not until the witness, awareness becomes aware of itself, consciousness becomes aware of itself and stays aware of itself, that the ego drops and it drops. It's just not real. It just can't possibly be seen as real. It's like you've got clothes on, being identified with them. How ridiculous would that be? Well, once awareness becomes aware of itself, that's how the mind sees it is ridiculous to be someone when you're not. You are pure awareness, you have always been pure awareness, you cannot be anything other than pure awareness, and you are here, right now.

~

S: Namaste Vishrant, I'd like to know if changing career to where we use less thinking and more physical activity will help?

V: Maybe, maybe. It depends on what you're actually involved in. I was involved in publishing in the 80s and I found that it was too hectic, too demanding, too heavy. I'd become like a war machine in a lot of ways and it was definitely in the way of my spiritual growth, my consciousness rising, so I gave it away and took up some things that were more useful in higher consciousness. I moved into service, becoming a naturopath and a psychotherapist. I moved into being in service which didn't involve so much of the mind. It was less intense, less stressful, working simply for myself and not having a huge staff which I had as a publisher – much easier for me to be more involved in the Way of the Heart and more involved in self-inquiry. Though during that period, I also had a family that I raised and the practise of openness, practise of acceptance, the practise of self-inquiry, and the practise of meditation all helped. Whatever you practise, you get good at. If you don't practise, you won't change, that's for sure. We just stay true to whatever default patterns we've got. It's up to you. You're in charge. You create your thoughts. You're the author.

~

S: What are the qualities of a surrendered mind?
V: It's not there. It's quiet, surrendered. Mine is silent. It's very quiet, very, very quiet. It's not moving. So you're awake. But the mind is quiet. It's resting.

~

S: Will acceptance to being abused or raped lead to higher consciousness?
V: Acceptance of anything teaches us surrender. You see, we can't actually learn surrender by itself, because surrender is actually a non-doing, so whatever happens to us in this life that is negative or seen as negative can be used to practise acceptance. Acceptance leads to surrender. It's how we learn surrender. Life can be horrific for human beings, but it's only in

the practise of acceptance that we learn surrender. The more things that go wrong, the more things that don't go our way, the harder our life is, the more we can practise, if we choose to practise. If we choose to resist, well, we just create suffering, and usually that doesn't change anything, but if we choose to accept, we start to learn unconditional surrender and this will take us home. It's up to you. The moment you turn yourself into a victim of anything, you go into resistance, you create suffering for yourself. It usually doesn't change anything. But if instead of turning yourself into a victim, you start accepting life as it is, the mind is learning something new, something invaluable because it's learning how to surrender. And surrender is the key to Enlightenment from the mind's perspective.

~

S: Some masters say we need to strive for Enlightenment with everything we have. And then others will say that the whole effort is futile, because we are it now. Is it about realising our true nature through radical acceptance and surrender?

V: If you don't give it your totality, you won't wake up. It's that simple. And the truth is, of course, you're already Beingness, but you don't know that. You're not aware of it because awareness is not aware of itself. So ultimately, they're telling the Truth, but from the mind's perspective, which is what most people live as or think they live as, if you want to wake up, you have to give it your totality because partiality doesn't work in any endeavour in life. What works is totality, nothing less.

~

S: Is there a value in having out-of-body experiences for Enlightenment? If yes, then how can one do it while meditating?

V: It's just more curiosity for the ego. It's just entertainment for the ego. And the ego is the thing that's in the way, the "I" is in the way. It's just entertainment. There's no entertainment in Beingness for the ego because it's nothingness. It's emptiness. It's vast. Ego is interested in past lives, out-of-body experiences, remote viewing, astrology, all sorts of things. It's just entertainment. Realms, oh, yeah, that's a good one. It just entertains the ego more and more and more. The ego needs to learn to get out of the way. Self-inquiry will do that. Who's aware? Who's aware of what you're thinking? Who's aware of what you want? What's aware? What's aware? Find that that's aware. It's the only thing worth doing.

~

S: I have been listening to so many of Oshos' discourses for almost the past two years and I enjoy it so much. I feel that it has accelerated my growth. Is it helpful to listen to so much of his discourses?

V: I listened to Osho's discourses also and I listened to his discourses for nearly 20 years because I love him. He was my master and listening to his discourses changed my life immeasurably. It turned me into a true seeker.

~

S: When one is practising self-inquiry, how can one tell if the attention is going back on the ego or it is going back on awareness?

V: It's good to do it with someone who's awake. Someone who's a teacher who can show you. But you can't really know if you haven't experienced it before. When awareness goes back on itself, there's a sense of silence, a sense of stillness, a sense of expansiveness. There's a certain emptiness and nothingness to it.

Unfortunately, the ego can produce those things with its imagination to some degree and so the best thing is to self-inquire continuously for long periods of time. Any thought that arises, you inquire into the thought. What's aware of this thought? What's aware? What's aware? What's aware? And you keep turning it and turning it and turning it and then bang: awareness may discover itself, an accident may occur and you find yourself as that stillness, as that silence, as that nothingness, as that vastness, as that emptiness. Keep self-inquiring. Don't stop. I recall Ramana Maharshi being asked the question "When should I stop self-inquiry?" And his answer was so lovely: when there is nobody left to inquire.

~

S: I've heard you say we all run true to default patterns. What patterns support higher consciousness and Enlightenment?

V: The pattern of being present to reality, which is present-moment awareness, and the pattern of being open, instead of closed. These two patterns support higher consciousness. And these two patterns are actually, in a lot of ways, against the way most people live. Most people live constantly dreaming, thinking somehow they're present to reality, but they're dreaming while they're being in the world. They're thinking, not being present to reality. Meditation every moment, being present to what is real, being open all of the time, always open, always open – these two patterns, which are basically patterns of the mind, can be developed through practice. It's up to you whether you're going to practise or not. If all you do is practise closure and defensiveness, you're going to live in suffering. If all you do is practise dreaming your way through the world, well, that's where you're going to be stuck because dreaming is lower consciousness. It's up to you. You're the one who develops the patterns through your practices. Practise openness, practise present-moment awareness, practise self-inquiry. Find out who you are.

~

S: How does someone rewire their patterns?
V: Through practice. It's the only way. There is no other way. If you are hardwired to be a certain way, closed, defended, the only way to change that is to practise openness, and if you practise it long enough, and you undo all of the defence systems, that will become your default pattern. But it takes quite a while to change. The default pattern doesn't happen quickly. Whatever we practise, if we practise long enough, that becomes our default pattern. Whatever patterns you're currently running are default patterns that you've practised for your lifetime. Those patterns can be changed, but only by doing something different than that for a long period of time. It's up to you.

~

S: What part of your mind did you find was the hardest to prepare for Enlightenment?
V: What was the hardest thing to let go? I guess it was the betrayal and rejection, being okay with that. You see, any belief system that we hold that has an expectation that creates contraction in us when that expectation is not met is basically in the way – having an expectation that people shouldn't betray me or shouldn't reject me, having an expectation that they shouldn't cause contraction when it wasn't met. So I removed that belief system because I didn't want to contract. I didn't want to create suffering in myself because of a belief system that was actually out of touch with reality because the truth is people do betray, they do reject. You do it yourself.

That was one of the harder ones to remove because underneath that particular one there was a lot of wounding from childhood which had to be dealt with. You deal with wounding by allowing yourself to feel it. In healing that wounding and undoing that belief system, there was a lot of freedom because I no longer had a belief that people shouldn't betray me or reject me. There's no contraction if they do and there's no wounding there because it's all been healed, a long time ago. It's up to you. If you're not willing to feel your wounding, you won't heal it. And if you're not willing to undo the belief systems that cause contraction in you, well, you will keep contracting. It's up to you.

~

S: Sometimes I struggle with just one thought. It will be something that continues picking at me, and this can go on for months. How do I discern between intuition or fears and worries?

V: I'm not seeing the correlation here between the one thought and intuition and worries. I love the present moment. I got into being present when I was a kid. I never really enjoyed dreaming that much, living in my head. It makes people incompetent. It kills your clarity. And so, I've always loved present-moment awareness. Some people call that meditation because it is being in the moment, present to what is real. And then whatever comes, comes. I don't think living in your head is a good place to live. I think it's a place where most people hurt themselves. Why not live in reality, have awareness on reality? It's sweet. It's pretty cool. I remember when I was younger, I used to do a lot of sports that were dangerous, extreme sports. It took me a while to realise that all I was doing was forcing myself into the moment because when you're doing something dangerous, like racing motorbikes or hunting sharks underwater or whatever, you actually are very, very present because of the danger level. It wasn't until I started meditating at the age of 28 that I realised I'd always been looking for meditation. I'd always been looking for being present to what is real because it's nice.

~

S: How does one open the lower three chakras to prepare the body for awakening in the heart chakra?

V: I don't know why there's a concern about the lower three chakras. Why not just open the Heart chakra, the third eye and the crown and see what happens?

The lower chakras belong to lower consciousness in a lot of ways. If you're really interested in higher consciousness, open your crown, open your third eye, open your Heart chakra and see where it takes you. I don't think there's a great deal of need to worry about the lower chakras. Open your Heart, open the third eye, open your crown, and adventure begins.

~

S: Vishrant my fiancé wants me to ask you why you always wear white. We love you. Love from Peru.

V: So in being with Osho Rajneesh in the 80s and 90s, I got to study Ayurvedic medicine and Indian religions, and in that studying, I also moved more and more into the energy world which is what Ayurvedic medicine is about and the whole way of Ayurveda. In that, I discovered that certain colours hold certain energies, and the colour of white is a sattvic colour. There's three gunas, what they call gunas in Ayurveda, and that's the tamasic, which is very unconscious, sleepy-type energy, the rajasic, which is kind of active and maybe anxious, and then there's sattvic, which is clean, pure clarity.

Now, in the different colours, the colour of white is a sattvic colour, and I was interested in sattvic because it helps the mind stay clear. It helps the mind stay pure. I love white. I don't need to wear white, that's not a need, and from time to time I wear black, but when I was a seeker, I was looking for the percentages. Whether that was the type of food I ate, the type of music I played, the colour of the clothes I wore, the type of energy I hung out in, I was looking for the percentages to help raise my consciousness. Ayurveda and Ayurvedic medicine helped me with an understanding that there is a way to become more pristine, to have more clarity, to be more here, and the colour white is just one of those things that gives that little percentage. I hope that helps.

~

S: Some time back, I had asked you that I was asking the question "Who am I?" and directing it to my Heart centre and I was getting a lot of anxiety and headaches. You asked me to try asking "What's aware?" I have been trying that and now I feel whenever I've asked that question, I feel some kind of energy movement in my third eye and some pressure on my temples, so now should I take it as I'm doing it in the right way and continue this?

V: Well it sounds like you're opening the third eye and the crown chakra, which would indicate that awareness is probably becoming aware of itself at some level through the self-inquiry methodology you're using, so I would, I would say that you're on the right track. You just keeping inquiring and turn awareness back. "What's aware?" And then be quiet. You never answer that question. You just ask the question "What's aware?" and turn awareness back to itself. Now, a more advanced methodology is if you start to feel your crown chakra, put your awareness on it. It's your connection with the universe as the universe. Crown chakra is very beautiful. If it's starting to open, that's lovely. Keep opening it. If you can keep your awareness on your crown chakra you will find that you disappear and find yourself as everything. It's another way to Enlightenment. I hope that helps.

~

S: How does one open the Heart, third eye, and crown chakras?

V: So, with the Heart chakra, it's openness itself, openness from the mind. The only reason the Heart chakra is closed is because our minds are closed, if somehow we haven't dropped our defence systems. The Heart chakra opens up and stays open when the mind is open. It kind of follows suit, so if the mind closes, the Heart tends to close down. The more defended we are, the more closed we usually are in the Heart area. Being undefended, being vulnerable supports the Heart. Being open supports love.

As far as the third eye and the crown are concerned, my methodology was very simple. I used to go and hang out with the awakened gurus because in their presence I found that my third eye and my crown would start to open up because of the Buddha field they were carrying, and at some point, it opened up so much that it never closed, that it's always open, crown and third eye. That was through participation with awakened people, hanging out with them, asking questions, being in satsang. Now as far as other methodologies to open the third eye or the crown go, I don't really know, hasn't been my experience. If you can find someone who's awake to hang out with, to be near, that's the best thing you can do. If you want your crown and you're third eye to open, also if you want your Heart to open, because their energy field will support it.

~

S: What do you remember the most about Osho?

V: I remember that I love him. That's what I remember, and the gratitude that I have to him for his sacrifice. A lot of people don't understand that because they look at Osho and they see a man. Someone who's awake has sacrificed their life. You see, there's no such thing as selfish Enlightenment. For someone to have woken up and stayed awake, they have given their life up. They've given it to Truth and as a result of that they've become a light so others may see. So I know the sacrifice that Osho made. And I love him so much.

~

S: Is meditation enough to master the mind?

V: Witnessing the mind itself is enough to master the mind, yes. Because if you witness it, and become separate from it, you see it in its entirety which gives you the opportunity to either run programs or not run programs. When we're unconscious to how the mind is operating, when we're just caught in the dramas, we don't have any power to change anything. But in witnessing the mind, we get to see what is detrimental and what is good for us, and as a result, we can run what's good for us and remove what's detrimental. So witnessing the mind is absolutely brilliant. It is a way to Enlightenment. And it is one of the main methodologies that Osho Rajneesh taught. And so I learned that from him: be the witness. Be the witness and it allows you to be separate from everything, and in that separation, you get to see clearly. You have clarity. You're not caught in the emotionality of the dramas. You have detachment. It's absolutely brilliant. At some point, if you continue witnessing, you find you are just that pure awareness that watches, that is simply here, that's aware of itself. So witnessing is a complete and total way to Enlightenment. I recommend it.

Thank you for satsang. Good to see you bravehearts here today.

CHAPTER TWO

The Call to Enlightenment

S: Hello Vishrant, can you please talk about the Call to Enlightenment?
V: It's a funny subject to talk about because there's a thirst in some people to know the Truth and there's an absence of that thirst in other people, and those who have this thirst are curious. They want to know something that's a little bit different. They want to know something that's beyond their programming, beyond their belief systems, beyond what they've been educated to believe as possibly true. Unless you actually have that curiosity, unless you actually are interested, it's probably an impossibility to communicate what the call for Truth is.

I can remember back to when I was a kid. I was interested in God. I was interested in higher consciousness. I was interested in heaven and I was interested in what hell was, because of course I was brought up as a Roman Catholic. At some point when I was in my young teens, I wanted to become a priest or a Roman Catholic brother to teach. So there was always a calling there. There was always this interest in something beyond, something greater than just the mind and its story of itself.

In the beginning, there were an awful lot of beliefs passed to me and the curious mind started wondering, well, these are just beliefs, they're not my own direct experience. What's actually real? And it is the doubter in the spiritual seeker that has them seek the Truth and the Truth has nothing to do with belief systems, it has to do with your own direct experience of what is actually real. In seeking what is real, you start having to put all of your beliefs in the "maybe" column. You have to start approaching with a sense of doubt because it is only in doubt that we can find the Truth. If all we have is faith, there is no guarantee whatsoever what we have faith in – which is a borrowed belief system – is real. In seeking Truth, in practising meditation and practising self-inquiry, in practising openness, we start to get a taste of what is actually real, of what the sages have been talking about for thousands of years, and in that taste of reality, the thirst for Truth fires up.

It was very much in my relationship with Osho Rajneesh, Bhagwan Shree Rajneesh, when I originally joined him, that I started to find that silence and that stillness and that vastness while in his presence. I realised that there was another mountain to climb because I'd climbed the mountain of business, entrepreneurialism, and I'd got to the top of my industry and there was nothing there. You just succeed. So what? There's nothing there. Then there was this new mountain that was presented to me and this mountain was the mountain of higher consciousness or the mountain towards Enlightenment.

Attempting to approach that mountain with the same methodologies that worked in business didn't work because in business we get to succeed through totality and through resistance. We get to succeed by standing alone, actually, in resistance, with totality. In higher consciousness, we get to succeed by standing alone in surrender. It's very different. It's much harder. It's much easier to resist because we're programmed to resist by nature. We're not programmed to surrender. We're not programmed to accept. We're programmed to resist by nature, so in going for higher consciousness, in going for Enlightenment, we're actually going against nature because nature dictates that we survive, and we survive through resistance.

Surrender doesn't support survival at all, so someone who has woken up, someone who has raised their consciousness levels to that level, has defeated the survival mechanism of their own mind. This is where the true rebellion comes in, to rebel against your own mind and learn surrender. Take away all of the belief systems that don't hold water and just go for your own direct knowing, your own direct experiencing of what is real. It takes a fair bit because you're left with not knowing which way to go in a lot of cases. I was with a spiritual master, Osho, and he pointed the way and he pointed the way quite clearly. His methodology was witnessing, watching the mind instead of being involved in the mind. Just be the witness, just watch, just witness, just watch what's there and keep witnessing, and after that, witnessing is awareness. If you keep witnessing, you develop a detachment from the mind itself and you start finding yourself more and more as just the pure awareness of what is happening. Now we're back to reality. Now we're back home.

People think that they are the mind. They think they are the body. But no, it is this that's aware of the mind before the mind even begins; there is this that's aware, pure consciousness. This is what we are and this is always here. So in fact, we're always at our final destination. People think they are their mind and they believe what it's thinking to be true, so they're lost in a dream. They're not lost in reality, they're lost in a dream and believing the dream to be true.

Find what is aware of the mind and become aware of that. Turn awareness back to itself. Turn consciousness back to itself, and wake up to what is real, to your true nature. This is where the quest for Enlightenment, the thirst for Enlightenment, the call takes you to home, to what you really are. On that journey, you discover that you're not the mind. You can't be the mind because you start experiencing no-mind when you're a meditator and so how can you be the mind when you're still here? The mind is quiet. It's not moving. You're still here in the silence, so you're not the mind.

Well then, what are we really? What is actually here? What is always here is pure awareness. In witnessing the mind we get to see, first of all, that we're not the mind, and we also get to see through the mind. We see the obstacles that the mind creates, and in seeing those obstacles, we can avoid them or change them. What we can't see, we can't do anything about, so insight is quite important. Some people think that insight is the answer and that's the end of it, but that's not true. Insight is actually an invitation to take the obstacles apart – they're in the way – or change them in some way that's better, if that's possible. Insight is not the answer by itself.

The call of this wanting-to-know-self-as-something-greater is an egotistical call in the beginning, but it doesn't end up that way because the further you go into consciousness, the higher your consciousness becomes, the less you are as an "I", the less you are as a something. Ultimately, you find yourself as nothing, vast nothing, vast emptiness, vast ... it can't be described what we truly are, but it has nothing to do with being a mind and a body. They are just vehicles that Beingness or existence or consciousness – whatever you want to call it – gets to witness out here. Before the mind begins, you are.

Are there any questions? Are there any statements? Are there any challenges to this teaching today?

S: Do you think it's a natural evolution to be attracted to Truth after a certain number of incarnations?

V: Incarnations? See, as soon as we start talking reincarnations, for a lot of people, we're talking about a belief system because they actually don't really remember their past lives. One of the things that I tried to avoid is giving anyone a belief system because from my understanding all belief systems are in a way traps. We're better off putting all belief systems in the "maybe" column and finding out through our own direct experience what is real and what is not real. So rather than actually explore that question and possibly give a lot of people another belief system, I'd rather not.

~

S: What exactly does the call to Enlightenment look like? Is there only one path?

V: Oh no, there's plenty of paths. For me it looked like wanting to become closer to God through being a Roman Catholic priest and brother and being in service when I was a teenager. I fell in love with Jesus as a child. I fell in love with his beauty, or the beauty that was being portrayed of him. I fell in love with the service that he offered humanity. I thought he was a kind man – a kind man who somehow was the son of God and that fascinated me, it was so interesting. It led me eventually to India to check out what the Hindus were talking about when they were talking about Enlightenment and what the Buddhists were talking about when they're talking about Enlightenment. It took me all over the world, to different places, this interest and this thirst in wanting to know who I am really, who I am really, rather than this thought that I'm a mind and a body.

I started to understand that in silence we find ourselves, and the ways to silence and stillness are meditation and self-inquiry and witnessing the mind. The practice of those things became prevalent in my life, looking to see what was real and what was not real and serving that that was real. I became a servant of Heart because I found that Heart was real.

Love was real. I became a servant from the mind's perspective. My mind became a servant of Truth, it became a servant of Heart, and in that service, it laid itself down because that's what works. What works is surrender. What works is unconditional surrender. The survival mechanism doesn't survive unconditional surrender. It's like a death. And in that there's so much freedom. There's no freedom really in scrambling around to survive.

I went to Murdoch University sometime in the early 90s and studied the old masters at the university because they've got a great library on spirituality, and reading, reading, reading, studying, studying, studying, I spent about six months there, studying all of the old masters whether they were Sufi or Buddhist or Hindu or Christian, for that matter, or Muslim. And the bottom line is all of the ones who were involved in Enlightenment all said the same thing. It all boiled down to unconditional surrender: let go, let go, let go. So now I understood the answer to every question around spirituality: let go, let go, let go.

~

S: Watching the mind does not seem possible. When I'm actively watching there are no thoughts, but when there are thoughts, the one who watches is one with them. How can I see the thoughts separately from the one that watches?

V: Okay, so that's not my experience at all. If my mind moves, it is witnessed. Most of the time it just stays still, but if it moves it is witnessed, and that was a habit that was developed a long, long time ago, some

30 odd years ago, from watching the mind instead of being involved in the story of the mind, being the witness of the mind. That practice began in meditation of just watching, sitting silently, doing nothing, and just watching. It took a while. It didn't happen straightaway. It took a while. It took a bit of practice, sitting silently, doing nothing, just witnessing. My understanding is that if you do that, if you sit silently, do nothing at all and just witness, you will find that more and more and more you are the witness rather than the mind. Then there's this separation. Now, what is witnessing? What is this that's witnessing? That becomes interesting. Before the mind was interesting, but what was witnessing? What is simply aware of the mind? This becomes more interesting. And what is it about? And so the mind is being used to turn awareness back to itself.

~

S: Why did our minds evolve from being humans' greatest advantage to our greatest problem?
V: I can't answer the question. I really don't know. I've got to go back 40-odd years, 48 years, because I started to realise when I was 20 that everyone suffers and everyone future projects to avoid suffering, or uses some other methodology of escapism to avoid suffering. I had to have a look at why, why is everybody suffering, and it's because we desire things to be different than how they are. Our addictive demand that things change creates suffering and our attachment to things that we have and our fear of losing them creates our suffering.

The whole world is suffering: the First Noble Truth, life is dukkha or dissatisfying. It took me a while to get that. I had a lot of trouble believing it because I was using all these escape methodologies. I was future projecting that "later" was going to be better, that everything was going to be okay when I got this, this, and maybe that. That was a lie I was telling myself because there's only now. What is it like now without using an escape methodology? If you watch your mind, you can see how it constantly wants things to be different. That in itself is a form of resistance and resistance is suffering. So I changed. I changed things. I stopped pursuing in that way. I started to see that the way we thought about the world created a lot of our suffering. Whenever we addictively demand that anything be a certain way, we create massive resistance in ourselves and that resistance is suffering and we don't actually have to do it. We can accept life as it is. "Such is life." This is the way it is. Or we can resist life and fight life and suffer until we die. I just didn't see the point in doing that. I didn't see the point in suffering at my own hand.

Then I was looking at – I think a little bit before 20 – I was looking at, well, what's the victim-orientated thinking? How does that come into play, where I actually start not taking responsibility for my feelings, but blaming situations, other people and even myself? What happens when I move to that mode is I suffer incredibly by being a victim of circumstance or other people or myself. I decided I didn't want to do this either. This suffering is created by me. Why would I want to be into suffering when I can stop doing that?

Then I started to have a look at worry, and I went wow . . . there's no advantage whatsoever in worrying. None. All you do is create resistance in your mind by procrastinating something you don't want to happen or you do want to happen over and over again. It changes absolutely nothing, kills your clarity, and creates suffering in you. I was lucky enough to discover these things because I was involved in a higher consciousness group or a personal growth group when I was 19 called Focal and Focal promoted a book by Ken Keyes called The Handbook To Higher Consciousness. I read it about 20 times because it was just gold. What do you think it's worth to not be a victim to life for 40-odd years? What do you think it's worth to not worry for 40-odd years?

Neither of those things has to happen. We do not have to support worry and we do not have to support any thought that creates suffering in ourselves. Watch your thoughts. Just witness them and see how when you want something to be different, it's a form of resistance. That resistance is actually a form of dissatisfaction which is suffering and we don't have to. We can be free of that if we want, if we put our minds to going, "No, I don't want to play that game anymore". Or you can continue.

This is one of the advantages of witnessing the mind: you get to see how the mind does all these things. You get to see how the mind creates its own reality with the way it thinks, and because you can see it, you can do something about it. If you can't see it, you can't do anything about it. It's not possible. It's up to you.

In watching – in just watching, sitting silently, doing nothing, and just watching – we start to find ourselves as that that is simply aware if we do it long enough. Now we miss it usually in life, because it doesn't move, and it is silent. And we're always looking for primal reasons, for something that moves and makes noise, yet what we truly are does not move and does not make noise and is always here.

~

S: Why has Osho given darshan to you and Shashank Anand and not his other lovers? Why is he still helping others even after leaving his body?

V: People look at Osho and they think of him as a person. Osho went way beyond being a person. He is living as Beingness, as all awakened ones do, and there is no difference. Beingness is Beingness. There aren't two Beingnesses. There's one Beingness. So Osho is here. Buddha is here. It's all here and you are here. We are all one. Teachings are the same because how can they be different? Just a little Westernised. The energy is the same. How can it be different? The Buddha field is the same. How can it be different? We are one. When awareness finds itself, a Buddha field is created. That Buddha field can be tasted anywhere in the world, but it always tastes the same. And the Buddha field created by someone who's awake is a doorway for you to find yourself as Truth. Osho is here.

~

S: What do we do when the mind becomes fearful and projects vivid thoughts of fear?

V: When fear arises, fear itself is a dream. It's not real. It might seem real because you're probably having some kind of physiological reaction such as adrenalin being fired into the system or acid filling the stomach getting ready for fight or flight. It is not real. Fear is not real. It's a projection. The moment we put our awareness on what is real, we start to decrease the power that the dream of fear has, but if all we do is put our awareness on the fear, it just ramps up.

If we take our awareness and put it on what is real – and everything is real but what the mind produces – we start to move away from fear and we start to remove its power. In becoming aware of what is around you, what is physically around you – the sights, the sounds, the smells – we are taking awareness away from fear and onto what is real. This works to bring us back to reality. In keeping our awareness on the fearful thoughts, we get to live as them because wherever our awareness is, that's what we live as. When we start moving our awareness more into what's real – the sounds, the smells, the sights – we're moving back to reality, we're moving away from this dream. This is the way to deal with fear.

There is another methodology that I use or used to use. I haven't used it for a long, long time. Whenever I was frightened of something, I allowed the worst to occur – whatever that might be. I was a diver in my day. I loved underwater diving and I was out boating every weekend. We have islands off the west coast of

Australia that are full of coral and fish and plants and all sorts of beautiful things to adventure, cave diving, all sorts of things. There are a lot of sharks out there as well so I used to dive knowing full well there were sharks and I was diving around the west end of the islands where there were sharks so I would imagine that it would be okay for the sharks to kill me and eat me. In allowing them to kill me, in surrendering my life, fear just dropped away because fear loses its power when you allow what you're frightened of to happen. It only has power while you're resisting it. Before I jumped into the water, I'd be okay with being eaten. I'd just give my life up, and in that, fear would drop away because it had been disempowered by my willingness to die which was the greatest fear, really.

So that was a methodology I used to use as well, but if we find people who are having panic attacks, the best way to bring them out of a panic attack is to have them put their awareness on something that is real, something that's actually happening, something around them, something they can see, something they can hear, and have them keep their awareness there. Then the power of fear disappears because they've come back to reality. Fear is only a dream. It's not real. I hope that helps.

~

S: When I do other things, I've got to stop focusing on my breath, so is it like an on-and-off practice on the breath? I'm confused on this issue.

V: Most human adults dream their life away, constantly thinking and having awareness on their thoughts. If you want to be a meditator, you start putting your awareness on the breath. That's a pretty good place to start because the breath is real and it brings awareness away from the dream. But it takes a lot of practice because if you're practised at living in your head and dreaming, it's going to take a lot of practice not to do that. We get to practise by putting our awareness on the breath. As we're sitting silently watching our breath, a thought might come in, so you deny the thought and come back to the breath. You stay with the breath. You stay with what is real. This is practising meditation. True meditation is being present to reality all of the time. That's true meditation. The practice of meditation is practising being aware of something that is real so you can be real instead of dreaming. Come back to reality. But it takes practice. It's not going to happen easily if you're a dreamer. Reclaiming reality from the dream that you found yourself lost in is going to take a lot of practice, but just keep in mind that up until the age of five, you weren't really that much of a dreamer, you were very present to reality, you were actually in meditation a lot of the time because you were present to what was real, what was around you, what you could hear. It wasn't until you went to school and learned to live in your head that you lost it all.

Meditation or the practice of meditation helps you reclaim reality from the dream that you've been lost in for probably a long time, but only with practice. You just keep practising, keep putting your awareness on what is real. When you keep awareness on what is real you find your whole life changes because when you're with what is real, there aren't any problems. Not really. Problems happen in your head. It's just what is. Up to you. You're the only one that can do the practice, nobody can do it for you and I won't say it's easy. If you're beginning and you've been a dreamer, it's going to be difficult. But wow, I recommend it. Reality really does rock.

~

S: Namaste Vishrant. Instead of putting awareness on something real when there is fear, can we face the fear and bring it very close to us?
V: We can do. The problem with that is there's a chance the mind believes the fear by having awareness on it. There is more chance of getting lost in fear and believing it to be real. Unfortunately, we live as wherever we put the totality of our awareness. If we're angry and we put awareness on anger, we live with anger. If we're sad, and we put our awareness on sadness, we live as sadness. If we're fearful, we put our awareness in totality on fear, we live as fear. Now, someone who's awake has awareness locked on awareness. Beingness is aware of itself. They live as Beingness. They live as pure awareness or consciousness. Wherever our awareness is at, that is where we live. I don't really recommend facing the fear. I'm not sure what you mean by facing the fear, but if it means putting awareness on it, I wouldn't go there.

Frightened of what? Frightened of sharks. I guess you could say that that's what I did when I jumped in the water with the sharks on the other side of the islands. I was facing my fears. But I wasn't entertaining them. I wasn't going "Ooh I'm going to get eaten by a shark here". As a matter of fact, I was just with reality. I'd jump in the water and be with the feeling of the water. I was listening to the bubbles because quite often I'd dive with tanks. I'd feel myself sinking because I was weighted. I'd be aware of the boat behind me. I'd be aware of the bottom coming up. There are so many things to be aware of. You don't have to be locked on to fear because the moment we lock on to fear with our totality, we get to live as it. Put your awareness on something else. And fear in itself is okay. There's nothing wrong with it. It's just part of the survival mechanism of the psyche. It's okay that it's there. You always begin with okayness. But you don't need to serve it. You don't need to focus on it. It's just part of the tapestry. There are lots of other things happening.

~

S: Where does the practice of self-inquiry take one after the awareness is turned to the one who is watching?

V: Okay, so Ramana Maharshi, a sage who died in 1950, was asked the question "When do I stop self-inquiry?" His answer was pretty good. He said, "When there is no one left to inquire" and I would tend to agree with that. Self-inquiry is a wonderful tool for turning awareness back to itself, and if awareness is on itself, there's no need to self-inquire, there's no need to ask "What's aware?" or "Who am I?" It's over. But if the awareness comes back to the ego, then the question arises, again, who is aware or what's aware of this, and hence turning it back again.

It's a process of continually turning awareness back to itself until awareness locks onto itself like two permanent magnets. And if it stays like that, that's Enlightenment. If it locks onto itself then it comes back to ego-based reality because awareness turns back to the mind solely, that's a satori, so there's been an experience of Truth as self. That's not Enlightenment, that's just a satori. In a lot of ways, it's an invitation to come home. Enlightenment is when that that is aware of itself, or that that is conscious, becomes conscious of itself, aware of itself and stays aware of itself. And when that happens a Buddha field is created in that human being, a field of energy that can be perceived by those who are sensitive enough to perceive it. This is the only real way to tell whether someone is awake or they're not awake, whether they have a Buddha field around them, and whether they have a Buddha field around them 24 hours a day, seven days a week.

It is possible for someone to self-inquire, find awareness on awareness and temporarily create a Buddha field, but then lose it because they go back to ego-based reality. Awareness is on awareness in someone who's fully awake 24 hours a day, seven days a week, and they don't live as an ego or a body anymore. They live as Beingness because their awareness is on Beingness, and we live, really do live wherever awareness is at. So when awareness is on itself, we live as reality. When awareness is on the mind, we live as this dream that thinks it's a somebody, but it's not. Take away your thoughts and who are you? And all thoughts are imagined, and we are not imagination, we are something, we are pure awareness, we are pure Beingness.

So endeavour to discover that by self-inquiring, meditating, practising openness – the practice of openness removes all of the obstacles that are in the way. Wonderful stuff. And self-inquiry turns awareness back to itself. Witnessing the mind allows you to become the witness and allows you to experience yourself as the witness. These methodologies work, but only if you practise them: not if you think they're a good idea, only if you practise them.

~

S: How does one differentiate between ego and awareness?
V: Hahaha, the ego is noisy. The ego is always noisy, and awareness is silent and still. It's easy to differentiate, because awareness doesn't think, to start with. It's silent. It's still. It's absolutely profoundly silent and profoundly still. The ego can't help itself. It's a noisy piece of equipment, so differentiation is pretty easy, really. Though the ego can pretend to be Beingness. It can pretend to be Beingness, but it gets very stale very quick when it's pretending. Beingness itself is always fresh, always in the moment.

~

S: In India, enlightened beings have been referred to as being twice-born. Can you please explain what this means?
V: Yeah. So, you're born through a mother and that is your animal birth, if you like, the body birth. Humans don't like to see themselves as animals often,

but they are. It's the animal birth and it's the birth of the spacesuit. The second birth is when they wake up because then awareness becomes aware of itself. That is an awakening and that is a new birth. But it's not really a birth either because all that's happening is you're becoming aware of what was always there. It was there before the body was born, but it is referred to sometimes as a second birth. Those who have woken up sometimes referred to it as a second birth.

For me, finding Heart was the best thing. At the age of 34, I found Heart and I considered that was an awakening. That was my birth. Before that, I felt that I wasted a lot of my life because I hadn't had Heart, I hadn't had love. Unconditional love is the true jewel of consciousness, and love, like Beingness, is always here, but often not perceived because human beings are too closed, too defended and too shut down. If we open right up, our minds open right up, love's here, we can see it, it's beautiful.

So as far as births are concerned, I considered that a second birth. And I feel like I'd wasted 33 years or 34 years of my life beforehand. Another birth is when you take sannyas, if you become a sannyasin to a spiritual master, and I took sannyas with my spiritual master Osho Rajneesh in 1983. And I considered that a birth. So being 68 now, I'm actually 40 years old from that birth. When you take sannyas, you take on a new name, you leave your past behind, and you take on a spiritual life, and that's very beautiful also.

Really, this double birth? Wake up and find out. Wake up and find out who you really are. Turn awareness back to itself. Use the mind to turn awareness back to itself. Then all the questions are answered.

~

S: Vishrant, disturbing pictures flash through my mind and I don't know why. How do you heal the unconscious wounds?

V: Yeah, difficult, but possible. It begins with acceptance. So the disturbing pictures flash through your mind. Instead of resisting them, accept them. That doesn't mean entertain them. It means accept them. In acceptance, our resistance to what is changes and our suffering changes.

Getting help from people who are further ahead is always a wise decision. For myself, I was very, very fortunate in that I fell into the hands of people who were into higher consciousness when I was 19 years old and it changed my life immeasurably because these people were further ahead than I was and they showed me how to get further ahead.

As far as healing wounds is concerned, I was pretty wounded because I'd had a rough upbringing. I was carrying a lot of pain-body, but I discovered that in allowing myself to feel it rather than avoid it – which I'd done most of my life – in allowing myself to feel it, I started to heal it.

But there was another step and that was not to produce anymore. A lot of my wounding had been produced by things that had happened in my life, traumatic events and the belief systems that supported me being a victim inside of those traumatic events. So in removing victim-orientated thinking, in removing those thoughts, I didn't produce any more of the wounding. That's one of the things that people do, they heal wounding by allowing themselves to feel it, but then they go and reproduce it again by running the same old story in their head and being a victim and just creating the same wounding again.

So there are two things that are involved in healing wounds. One is: don't recreate it again by being a victim to anything ever; and then allow yourself to be tenderly okay with whatever is appearing. If it's pain, you be tenderly okay with it. If it's sadness, whatever, whatever it is, you be tenderly okay with it and everything will empty out. All of the pain bodies will empty out, if you are willing to feel. We heal by feeling, and that's up to you. No one can do it for you. You have to go on that adventure yourself. Not necessarily by yourself though. There are people out there who can help you. There are therapists out there who can help you. And these people are worth saying hello to.

~

S: A follow up question from the last question: in reference to disturbing pictures flashing through the mind, is this unconscious wounding or an undisciplined mind?

V: I think I have not met a human yet who isn't wounded or hasn't been wounded. I think we're all wounded and we're all badly programmed. When we talk about unconscious and conscious and we start looking at our programming, we get to see that wow, we swallowed an awful lot of belief systems that weren't real. We've been brainwashed.

Higher consciousness in a lot of ways is reverse engineering the mind's programming and going through it and going "No, no, no, not this one, not this one, not this one," because it's rubbish. Letting it all go, seeing through the mind and allowing ourselves to feel what's there, allowing ourselves to really feel it, to be with it, to be tenderly okay with it instead of using every diversion technique known to man to avoid our pain, we can heal it and not produce anymore.

Stop producing pain. Stop being a victim to life. It's a choice. You actually have to volunteer. A bad thing can happen, but you have to volunteer to be a victim of it. It's just what is. This attitude works, but you have to practise it. No one's going to do it for you. There may be some people who can advise you on the subject, but you basically have to do it. Nobody healed Vishrant's' wounds but Vishrant by allowing whatever was there to be okay, tenderly okay, and by not topping up the wounding by being a victim to this, that, and everything else. This is the way. It's up to you. I don't know any magic pill that's going to work. You have to feel your wounding to heal it and you have to stop wounding yourself by running victim-orientated stories about life. Your choice.

~

S: Sir, have you been contacted by any astral being?
V: What makes you think I'm not one? Tune in. See what's here. You won't find anyone here. There's a voice talking, but there's nobody talking.

~

S: How should one deal with competitiveness in the workplace and trying to protect oneself from others when trying to practise openness?

V: Well, it's easy: be on their side. You see, the moment we're only on our own side, in any kind of situation, we've basically gone to war. Competitiveness itself is a form of warfare. Have a look at it. If you really want to play the game sweetly, be on their side as well. Always be on the other's side. Always, always, always. It changes the whole gestalt. Even if you're in an argument with your partner, be on their side as well as your own. Hold them in tenderness as well as yourself and you'll find it changes everything. The moment we are only on our own side, we've gone to war, and unfortunately with war, Truth is usually the first casualty. Make yourself available to be on everyone's side and on your side. This is a beautiful way to live life.

~

S: Are we not foiling the consciousness game by getting out of it by obtaining Enlightenment?

V: You can't become enlightened unless you've got superconsciousness. It's not foiling the consciousness game, it's the top of the mountain. It's the aim, to sit at the top of the mountain and stay there and see everything happening. Higher consciousness is really just the consciousness of everything the mind is doing – being okay with everything it's doing, seeing everything it's doing, not being ignorant at all, not being caught in it at all. The ultimate in higher consciousness of the mind is unconditional acceptance of what is, and that leads to superconsciousness which is awareness that's aware of mind becoming aware of itself and staying aware of itself. The ultimate in higher consciousness is superconsciousness.

So from my perspective, there is lower consciousness, there is higher consciousness and there is superconsciousness. Lower consciousness is the ignorance of dream. Higher consciousness is you're not dreaming anymore, you're just really present and you're aware of what your mind is up to all of the time so you're not lost in anything. And then superconsciousness, one step above higher consciousness, knowing self as Truth. Awesome, and it's up to you. You can put yourself in any level you want with the way you think and what you do in the world. But if you really want to wake up, self-inquire, meditate, practise openness, and hang out with people who are awake. That's a good one.

~

S: What happens if you turn your back on Truth? Would the call always be there?

V: Yes, I did have that experience. I had a disagreement and I fell out of friendship for a while with my spiritual group, the Rajneesh organisation in 1985, and I turned my back on Truth for about six months. The way I avoided the call for those six months was by partying, really. I partied hard and had a lot of fun and managed to avoid everything. Then I went into a place where I normally went to party and I asked the staff where a friend was who I used to party with and he said, "Well, he's died." I said "What do you mean?" "Well, he's committed suicide."

He was such an up, bubbly character. It was just hard to depict him as someone who would even consider killing himself, but he did. And in that moment, the realisation and the recognition again of impermanence and that we can go beyond the mind, we can wake up here, was so strong that I went and took sannyas again. I got my sannyas back and turned my life back to spirituality because I was way past the point of no return. I knew too much.

When you know too much about higher consciousness, about superconsciousness, it's really hard to turn your back on it without you hurting yourself somehow. Being in denial, trying to blind yourself, trying to become ignorant again is very difficult and it's painful. Once you start this journey of higher consciousness you should complete it. You don't want to stop halfway. You keep going.

It was relatively difficult to get my sannyas back, but I did because at that time I had an understanding that Osho Rajneesh was a doorway to superconsciousness, a doorway to Enlightenment, and that he was teaching a methodology and a Way of the Heart that would end up there. It was like coming back to my love affair with Truth, coming back to my love affair with Osho. Coming back to my love affair with life itself. I don't think it's good for people to turn their back on Truth, especially if they've gone too far. They live in some form of denial and I think that ends in bitterness.

S: How should one go about looking for awakened people locally? Do long-distance relationships work?
V: You know, I don't think there's that many awakened people. Someone who is enlightened has a Buddha field and if they don't have a Buddha field, it doesn't matter what they're saying, and as far as Buddha fields are concerned, they're relatively rare. You'll hear about it, someone who's holding satsang. You'll hear about someone holding that field of energy. You'll hear about it and you can go along and check for yourself. If that field of energy is there you'll know you're dealing with someone who's awake. If the field of energy is not there, they're not awake and they're probably a waste of time because someone who is not awake can't help you wake up. They can't even wake themselves up.

So it's always best to find someone who is awake and preferably someone who is walking their talk – someone who is actually living what they're teaching. That can be done through Zoom, through video, through online live things. I've found that to be true. This is a relatively new phenomenon which is pretty cool. Ideally, it's best to be in person with someone if you're looking for a physical master. Be in person with them because they'll help you wake up. They'll show you the way. They'll show you the obstacles. They'll show you everything that you need to see, and if you're willing? Well, that works.

If you're not willing, if you want to do it your way, well that probably won't work. If you're lost in the jungle and you come across a guide who's going to guide you out, you follow the guide. You don't say it's better to go that way, you follow the guide. Otherwise, you stay lost. But you've also got to make sure that the guide knows the way out, and when it comes to Enlightenment, the only one who knows the way out is someone who is awake, and they have a Buddha field. Sit with them, watch how your mind goes quiet. Watch how your mind expands. Watch how you find you're descending into stillness. The Buddha field is beautiful. It in itself is the Buddha and it's the doorway into your own true self.

Thank you for satsang. Good to see you bravehearts here today.

CHAPTER THREE

How Do I Get Free of Suffering?

S: How do I get free of suffering?
V: I think it's not a bad idea to actually get a definition of what suffering is first. Quite often people think that discomfort or pain is suffering, but discomfort is discomfort and pain is pain. Our suffering commences when we resist discomfort or we resist pain. We've got to look at what suffering actually is. If you don't want to suffer, don't resist. That's way easier said than done, but that's the bottom line. If we suffer, it's because we are resisting life in some way. We're resisting something that's not going our way that we'd like to be different than how it is. We're addictively demanding something to be in some way different and in that addictive demand there is suffering because we're in resistance.

We live in a society that suffers because we're all programmed to resist life. It's actually part of survival. It's a part of the survival mechanism of the mind to resist, but it doesn't need to be so because we're intelligent, we can actually learn to accept life as it is rather than resist life as it is, but that's up to us. To go against our original programming is pretty difficult, but it's absolutely possible. You think about it. Pain is just pain. Discomfort is just discomfort.

Suffering only occurs when we resist those things, and if we don't resist, we don't suffer.

The question, how do I stop suffering? Stop resisting. Life is going to be the way life is. Things aren't going to go your way all the time. You are going to lose practically everything you ever have, because we eventually die. If we resist, we suffer. If we accept life as it is and we trust that what's happening is supposed to be happening – otherwise it wouldn't be happening – we can live in trust, there is no more suffering. There may still be pain, there may still be discomfort, but the suffering is over because we're not resisting anymore. You have to have a look at your process, at how your mind is operating. Are you resisting or are you in acceptance of life? Are you making things okay or are you making them not okay? And of course, you're responsible for that. Nobody's doing that to you. You create your thoughts. Nobody creates them for you.

Your reality, in fact, is created by you and the way you think. Life is just the way it is. If you can trust that life is the way it is and that things are happening the way they're meant to be, you can have a pretty cruisy life even though you might lose everything. But if you resist, wow, you're gonna suffer, that's a fact. Acceptance is the key to having a happy life: acceptance of what is, and then we can stay cool, then we don't get uptight. It's just what is. The good, the bad, and the ugly is just what is. It is a beautiful way to live with this understanding and operating this way. Have a look at what happens inside of you.

When you go into disagreement with life, disagreement with people, disagreement with situations, what actually happens inside of you? Witness your own mind and see, see what it's up to. In the witnessing, we get to see that we create our own reality and that we don't need to resist.

We can find ways to accept that does not make us impotent. We can still change things from a place of acceptance. Because really acceptance is a place of openness and we can still make a difference in the world from a place of acceptance. We don't have to go into resistance inside of ourselves to make changes. That might be what you believe, but it's not true. We can do everything from openness. We can do everything from non-resistance. This is the Way of the Heart, the way of non-resistance. This is the way of love because we perceive love when we're open and we're open when we're not resisting life. All resistance, all defence systems are in the way of us perceiving the most beautiful thing that's here, love. The endeavour for the seeker is not just to find themselves as Truth, but it's to teach the mind to stop resisting life.

Any questions, any statements, any challenges to this teaching today?

S: Is it actually possible to never suffer again?

V: Heck yeah, if you're not resisting life you're not suffering. I have to categorise it. It does not mean you mightn't feel pain because you probably will. It doesn't mean you won't feel discomfort because you probably will, but you're not resisting so you're not suffering. To learn not to resist takes a fair bit because we're programmed to resist both causally and primarily through our genetics, but because we're intelligent we can learn to accept life as it is. We can learn to not resist. We can learn to support the Way of the Heart which is the path of non-resistance. But that's up to you.

~

S: Is it true that what we resist persists?
V: I don't know. I don't see any point in resisting. I really don't.

I got to look around myself when I was a teenager in my late teens. I saw that so many people were suffering and there wasn't anything happening. They would just turn themselves inside their own minds into victims of situations, victims of other people and victims of themselves. They were going into resistance against what is instead of accepting what is. And it was way back then that I decided that I wasn't ever going to support victim-oriented thinking in myself and I wasn't ever going to support worry in myself – or procrastination, another form of resistance – because there's no positive outcome to it. There's nothing to it, except you suffer. Stop it. You have the power.

~

S: Is there a place for facial hair in a spiritual journey?
V: Well, I love your question. I really don't know. The spiritual journey has nothing to do with the body. It has everything to do with going inside and finding yourself as pure awareness or Truth and Truth

doesn't have facial hair and neither does love. The body does. The good news is we are pure awareness and we are not the body and we are not the mind. Before the body and mind, we are. We already are before the mind even begins. We are that that is purely aware, everything that is consciousness, and it doesn't necessarily have any facial hair *laughing* Why do you ask this question?

S: It's just that everybody who's on the path seems to have like a long beard and long hair. So I was just wondering if that ties into some kind of like a spiritual practice of being tolerant of this hair and living with the discomfort or anything like that.

V: I really don't know. I prefer to keep the hair here short. I don't have to do much to it you know and the beard's recently trimmed as well because I'm not big on having to care for it. It's like you have long hair and it takes a lot of maintenance. It's much easier to have short hair. But this is simply pragmatic.

My teacher Osho Rajneesh had a very long beard. He didn't have much hair. He'd lost it. He'd gone bald, but he had a very long beard and he was very beautiful to look at. I imagine having a long beard would have been reasonably high maintenance. At some stages of my life, I have had long beards and they took a fair bit of work, you know. I don't think it's holy to have a lot of hair on your face. I don't think it's not holy either because I really don't think there's anything that's holy. Spirituality is not holy, just finding yourself as Truth is reality. What spiritual seekers are looking for is what's real: reality.

It's not holy. It's just what we are which happens to be everything, and when awareness turns onto itself, we discover that to be Truth, that we are everything and nothing. And if we're surrendered enough, or open enough, we perceive love and that love is not holy either. It's always here, but a lot of people don't perceive it because they're too closed. That's all.

So as a reality teacher, I teach people how to open up so they can perceive love. I teach people how to turn awareness onto itself, so they can find themselves as Truth. To me, this is just reality. What's not real is the constant dreaming that people do, the constant thinking they do, you know, that's what's not real. As a matter of fact, just about everything's real except what you think. What do you reckon?

S: Yeah, makes sense. The last time I talked to you, you told me to try practising just sitting, so I've been trying to just sit and not do anything. I was just wondering if there is a minimum amount of time that you would suggest or duration of time that I should continue doing that and is there value in it?

V: Okay, so now that you've got to sitting, watch your mind. Just be the witness of your mind and what will happen is, as you sit and you watch the mind, you'll start to get distance from your mind, you'll start to see it as something separate. You're moving more towards being the pure awareness of it than you are being in the dream of it. And so sitting is lovely. Now, watch the mind, just witness the mind as though you're watching someone else's mind, without judgment, and you'll find you get detached more and

more and more. And you'll find more and more and more peace as more and more detachment occurs.
S: Thank you so much. Thanks. Good to talk to you.

~

S: Did you know to not resist and stop suffering in your previous lives?
V: Yes. This is one of the things that the West doesn't get so much. We've done this before. And whatever merits or whatever practices that we've been involved in, in the past, good or bad, can come through to the next life, and I remember doing these in many lives. Yes.

~

S: Do you always know when you are suffering?
V: Some people don't know. They're so used to suffering that they don't even realise they're suffering. They're so used to it. It's such a pattern, they don't even recognise that they're suffering. If I was to suffer, I'd definitely know because I don't suffer, but if you're suffering all of the time because you're constantly resisting life from the time you get up until the time you go to bed, you probably don't even notice your suffering. I got to be quite still when I was young. I got to be left alone for long periods of time and I got to watch my own mind and see what it was doing, what it was up to, and how people create the mess in themselves by overthinking everything by worrying, by just problem solving constantly. The present moment is quite beautiful until you bring something into it that's not. A negative thought maybe? A problem maybe? A worry maybe? But

you're doing that. Life is just the way life is. You create your reality.

S: Do you think it is a human pattern to be comfortable in suffering?

V: Unfortunately, I think it is, yes. When people suffer a lot because of their own resistance, they need to find relief from that from time to time so they get into overeating or drugs or alcohol, gambling, gaming – they get into anything. They get into religion – anything that will take them away from the moment. In the moment, they're suffering because they're resisting life.

If we look at different religions, some religions sell hope of a future which is just an opiate taking you away from the moment. It's popular because people are suffering in the moment because they're resisting life, but really the future doesn't exist. Hope is rubbish. There is only now and it is always now. If you live in the future now, in these projections now, you'll be living in them later, because it'll be your habit and you'll miss these beautiful moments that are here now because you're thinking about later, projecting to later, postponing to later. That's crazy, if you ask me.

~

S: Is a cloudy mind or a non-clear mind a symptom of suffering?

V: It's a symptom of a lot of different things, mostly procrastination. How do we get an unclear mind? Well, all you've got to do is overthink anything. Worry, procrastination, problem solving – anything that keeps us locked in our minds creates a density of energy which kills our clarity. The best thing we can possibly do is have awareness on reality, have awareness with what is real rather than what is not, which is what we're thinking. The only thing that's not real is this. Meditation is being aware of what's real. That's all it is. I love meditation and meditation just means being present to reality. I love it. It's awesome. It is not so pleasant to be present to what you're thinking because we've all been programmed at school to be problem solvers. Where's the joy in that, really? What about just being in life and celebrating life by being present to what is real, life itself?

~

S: There was an Indian guru named Guruji Sangat who has shown Om light emitting from his body to some of his devotees. What is its significance according to you?

V: Okay. When someone wakes up, there is an energy form produced called a Buddha field. It's a form of energy that emanates from here and goes out, outward, and it can be perceived by those who are sensitive enough to perceive it. Now this energy form in someone who's awake can also involve a great deal of energy going through the body and that energy going through the body can be perceived by some as light. It's just energy. The truth is what does it appear in? What does the energy that's appearing appear in? What is its background? Seekers can get caught very easily in light and caught in all sorts of spiritual phenomenon or caught in analysing their minds, but really, what is it all appearing in? What is this that is simply aware of all of this, whether it's light or darkness? What is this that's aware? Getting caught in the magic or the siddhis around spirituality is a trap. Not to say that people who are awake won't use those abilities to help people by lifting them, by clearing them or by lighting them up, but to actually just be interested in those is a trap. What are they appearing in? What is the background? What's aware of them? This is best.

~

S: Some meditations are to watch internal talk and imagination. Isn't that then a meditation or awareness on something that is not real?

V: That's true. So there are different types of meditation. One is just watching the breath which is real because the breath happens; it comes in and goes out, you're watching something that's real and you're actually abandoning the mind to do that. You're abandoning thought to do that. That teaches you to be present to what's real.

Another methodology is to watch the mind, to be the witness of the mind. In being the witness of the mind, you're developing a distance from the mind so you're getting to be detached from the mind. In that detachment, you start to find that you are the witness, that you are that that's purely aware of the mind and that the mind actually has nothing to do with you and never ever had anything to do with you. The same as the body has nothing to do with you. You are that that is aware of the spacesuit and its on-board computer.

There are different methodologies that will take you to different places. It is lovely to be present to reality because living in your head is not good. We were not programmed to be happy. We were programmed to be problem solvers and efficient little machines. Being present towards what is real is a huge advantage. Watching the mind, being the witness of the mind, allows you to start finding yourself as pure awareness. It's a methodology to Enlightenment, the same as self-inquiry. So there are different methodologies, and if you're with a spiritual teacher, they'll offer these different opportunities, different methods to find yourself as Truth. It's not about anything to do with the mind or the body really. It's about what's aware of it. Who are you? Really, what are you really? And then when you first start finding awareness ... and awareness, wow ... then you also discover that there's nobody here. And there never was: just a figment of the imagination of the mind that thought it was a someone.

~

S: I have a question about meditation, because I've done a fair bit over the years and there's been different suggestions made. Watching the breath is one of the classical ones and vipassana meditation. I did a mindfulness retreat with Chime Shore at the Origins Retreat Centre in Balingup and I started meditating with my eyes closed which I always have, and he said no, meditate with your eyes open. If you close your eyes up, you go to sleep. When you want to take meditation into the world, you have your eyes open.

So they teach meditation with open eyes. What's your comment on this?

V: For the first 10 years of practising watching the breath, which was my methodology also, I sat with my eyes open at a 45-degree angle to the ground to stay awake. And I sat in a half lotus position without a back support which also kept me awake. I found that in the early days, if I shut my eyes, I would just go into sleep and dream, but if I kept them open at that 45-degree angle, I was able to stay with my breath.

~

S: Hello. I'm struggling with some health issues that have been going on for almost three months. What do you recommend in order to heal this? Thank you.

V: Acceptance. I've been struggling with health issues for the last three months or so. I think its two months and three weeks actually. I came off a motorbike and broke my collarbone and four of my ribs and it has been one heck of a journey because for the first month and a half, two months, even breathing was painful, let alone getting up, moving around. But acceptance, it works. You just accept what it is. You don't complain to yourself. You don't complain to others. You just accept it. Whatever the illness is, whether it's physical or mental, you accept. In acceptance, we have killed suffering. We may still have pain. So every time I got up, I hurt, but I wasn't resisting it. I wasn't creating suffering by resisting the pain and that's the thing, when we can learn to accept life as it is or our illnesses as they are, whatever is there as it is, we stop suffering and our life becomes more beautiful. It's up to you because you're the one who's going to supply the acceptance or the resistance, not the world. You do it. So now when I take a deep breath out, just a little bit of pain, it's pretty good. It's getting much better and I can walk around reasonably well without pain. I can even get back on my motorcycle and ride for a while, not long, but a while before it starts hurting. The world we live in, our bodies, our spacesuits are fragile and eventually they're going to die. It's what is. If we can accept the process, life can be pretty cool.

~

S: Is it sometimes better to let people suffer and be where they're at in life in order for them to grow and learn from their experience?

V: You mean you have a choice whether you let people suffer or not? I think that people's suffering is done by them, not by your choices. So who lets who suffer? You're the one who creates your suffering. No one can let me suffer. I'm just not going to. It's your choice to suffer because you're the one supplying the resistance or the non-resistance. When I see people suffering, there's not much I can do about it. I know how they're creating it. It's what is. It's their karma. I could possibly tell them that they could accept life, but that's their choice, too. We all create our own reality. I see suffering every time I look at human beings because we live in a society that resists life while pretending to be happy. People thinking they'll be happy later when they get something different, when things change. Rubbish! There's only now.

~

S: The next question is from a viewer. How do I know if I'm tolerating something versus accepting?

V: Yeah, good question. Tolerating is still suffering. If you're in acceptance, the story is gone. The drama is gone. If you're in complete acceptance, it's over. If you're tolerating, that's a form of resistance, you're still suffering and you're waiting for something. You're suffering. You haven't hit full acceptance. You may have hit partial acceptance, but you haven't hit full acceptance because with full acceptance the story is gone. The drama is gone. Oh there might still be pain. Acceptance doesn't get rid of pain. It gets rid of the suffering because it gets rid of the resistance to pain.

~

S: As I become more meditative, I'm slowly losing interest in daily activities that I used to partake in. I feel very bored and that boredom leads me to distraction and away from meditation. Please comment.

V: Look, I love meditation, being present to what is real, because if you're present to what is real you don't get bored. You only get bored if you're still in your head comparing things. And so maybe you need to examine what boredom is and then see what you're doing, see what you're actually up to. If you're in the moment, you can't get bored. If you're present to reality, you can't get bored because you're not comparing, you're just here. It's all good. The other thing with boredom, if you do have boredom, is accept it and it loses its power. It's only when we resist boredom that it has power. It's only when we resist anything really that it has power. Stop resisting, be okay with what is, and put your awareness on what is real. If you're feeling like you aren't doing a lot of activities, go for a walk and walk with present-moment awareness of everything around you, with your breath, with your footfalls, with the sun, with the air, with the moon if it's out – anything but living in your head. Meditation really is just a recovery system. Recovers you from the dream you found yourself lost in since you left school because that's what happens when we go to school. We get taught how to dream. We get taught how to live in our heads so we can become little problem solvers, efficient little machines. Meditation is the antidote. The practice of meditation is the antidote. It takes you out of your head again and back into reality. It's brilliant. If you're getting bored, you're still in your head because that's a head thing. You're comparing somewhere.

~

S: You saw Osho live dancing. How was that?
V: Mind blowing. That was the type of experience that you can't even really describe. This awake being dancing and moving, yet you can feel that there's nobody there. It is bizarre. And the way he danced, he was playing with energy. He was directing energy and so he was blowing people's minds. It was fantastic. He was really a wonderful master.

~

S: Talking about dancing, I've always loved dancing and what you've said about if you're really in the dance the "I" disappears. I think it was in Pune when they did

Sufi dancing, and when you spin around, it comes to that point when you are still and it's the world that's spinning. It's like those are satori moments and they're just so beautiful. Did you ever do the Sufi dancing?

V: Yes, I did a Sufi group in Pune at the Rajneesh Mystery School and I did a month of whirling. We whirled every day, all day long, and yes, you become the centre and the world moves around you. You become the silent place, the still spot. Very nice – and then you'd fall down at the end and the world would keep spinning around, but you were the still spot that was lying on the floor.

S: I remember that they used to say to us that when you finish, you bow down. And you do that for about 10 seconds and that way you lose the dizziness.

V: Yes, we spun for way too long. We'd spin for hours and hours on end and you didn't bend down, you fell down.

S: Oh that's wonderful. So many parallels or synchronicities I get when I listen to you. You were talking about your motorbike accident. Well, there was a period of about two years when I had five or six falls and because I wasn't into resistance, I got very little damage. I got a bruised rib one time and a frayed shoulder one time, but it was like, if you resist, you get much more hurt than if you just allow it.

V: Yeah, they reckon drunks fall over and don't hurt themselves so much, they're so loose. I've heard this too. Not that I would have ever experienced that. Look one time, in Pune, I went out and saw a guru. He was quite a way out of Pune and I had to go by rickshaw. I think it took an hour to get out there to see him. I sat with him for an hour and I said to him, "Well, I'm interested in Enlightenment". He says, "Everything's going well, you need to go away now" so I left thinking "Oh gosh, that wasn't much fun". And that night they found me. I'd lost my memory completely. That night they found me wandering around the city of Pune dancing wildly like I was drunk and I hadn't had a drink. This guy blew my mind and lit me up in such a way that I was roaming around Pune drunk – drunk on something, but it wasn't alcohol. It was just energy, you know. My mind had been blown and was just empty.

S: We miss the energy when we get too caught up in thinking, don't we?

V: Well, that was the attraction to Osho. He had a beautiful energy field. People would come and sit in his presence and get blown away. Unfortunately, they got addicted to the energy field, the Buddha field, and they didn't do the work on themselves, which is what they needed to do. They needed to sort out a mind that would support higher consciousness, but they didn't. A lot of them didn't. They just became addicts to the energy field. I became an addict to the energy field, but I was interested in Mystery School so I did a lot of Mystery School stuff. I did a lot of working on having a look at what was going on here.

S: Like you, I've spent a fair amount of time with Teertha, or Paul Lowe as he is known now. I did two workshops with him in Bali and they were really powerful.

V: Yeah, Paul was one of my main teachers. I was with him in '84 for four months in America, in Oregon, and then four months in '85 with him in America, and then five months in Italy with him in '87. He was one of the major influences in my life. I have got a lot of gratitude for that man.

S: Yeah, same here. Thank you. Thank you.

~

S: Should I skilfully manipulate people into suffering a little less or just accept their suffering?

V: [LAUGHING] Skilfully manipulate people into suffering less? Wow. I give people a choice: resist life and suffer or accept life and don't. Your choice. There's no manipulation required. It's your choice. You choose.

~

S: How do I know that I have done my job well? I am a perfectionist and I'm never satisfied. I always feel like I can do more and better. How do I come out of this pattern?

V: Okay. You have to see the perfection of life as it is. You're not going to survive anyway. None of us are. The body doesn't survive, it dies. Everything is perfect exactly as it is. We don't need to improve anything really. We are perfectly broken as we are. The need for perfectionism is going to drive you absolutely batty. If you can find a way to accept life as it is, you can find peace, but if you're trying to create perfectionism, everywhere you go, you're going to find nothing but tension. You're creating this, nobody else. Have a look. Everything is actually okay as it is and it's okay for us to fail. It's okay for us to succeed too, but it's okay for us to fail, because in the big picture, it just doesn't matter. It just doesn't matter.

~

S: Vishrant, I've had many young clients over the years in their 30s and 40s that have had health issues that lead to hardcore anxiety. Are they just scared to die young?

V: Yeah. Yes, they are scared to die young and if we can become willing to die, we can be free but as long as we are clinging to our life, as a matter of fact clinging to anything, we are actually stuck in lower consciousness. In the willingness to die, we become free. Unconditional surrender is a death of the 'I'. It's a death and unconditional surrender facilitates enlightenment. As long as we're clinging to anything, the harder we cling, the more we suffer because we're offering resistance to what is. We're resisting and we're all terminal. I came to an understanding of this when I was very young because I was a martial artist and I did full contact martial arts. If I was frightened to die or frightened of being hurt, I would've never been able to fight because fighting is dangerous. Full contact martial arts are dangerous. I became willing to die and in the practice of being willing to die I found so much freedom from fear because if you're willing to die fear no longer has power. Unconditional surrender is awesome. It is the key to higher consciousness and enlightenment. It is also the key to heart. So, you yourself surrender unconditionally, wake up, be alive so, others can see.

~

S: Sir, have you heard about Krishnamurti? What are your views?

V: There are a few Krishnamurtis. I understand that the Krishnamurtis are awake. I understand that. I find them a little bit too heady for me. I'm more into the practices rather than listening to people talk about spirituality or higher consciousness.

For me, I recognised quite early that the collecting of knowledge doesn't make your consciousness levels rise. What makes your consciousness levels rise are spiritual practices: the practice of self-inquiry, the practice of meditation, the practice of witnessing the mind, the practice of surrender, and the practice of yoga. Asanas can actually open you right up. Thinking about it doesn't do much. Understanding it doesn't do much. As a matter of fact, I think understanding is a big booby prize in spirituality. What works is practice, and so when it comes to Krishnamurti, I recognised that they were awake, but I wasn't that interested in just listening to stories about Enlightenment or stories about spirituality. I was more interested in doing the practices because it's only in practice that we get free, not in thinking about it or understanding, and a lot of people get trapped in this. A lot of spiritual people get trapped in this because they think that if they study and they learn about spirituality, they learn all of the sutras, they study the Buddha, they study all of this stuff that somehow they're going to raise their consciousness levels and get enlightened. No, that's not true. You can't educate yourself to Enlightenment. You can practise surrender, you can practise openness, you can practise self-inquiry, you can practise meditation and you can practise witnessing the mind. Practice brings you home, nothing else.

~

S: Life is dissatisfying, but you are not dissatisfied. Does that mean you have no life?
V: There's nobody here to be dissatisfied. There's nobody here. What happens when awareness finds itself is satori. What happens when awareness stays on itself? The "I" drops. There's no sense of anybody being here. There's talking, but there's no sense of anybody talking. There's the movement of the hand, but there's no sense of anyone moving the hand. That is all gone. It has dropped. The one that gets dissatisfied left the building.

~

S: How do you raise a child to not suffer in this life? Where would you start with this task?
V: Well, I raised three children. And two of them were raised in a Buddha field for most of their lives and they grew up to be wonderful people, but they still suffered because they hadn't learned to surrender yet. They hadn't learned to accept life as it is yet because they've learned from their parents, but they also learn from their peers. They learn from the church, they learn from the government, they learn from all of these different sources, not just you. In Australia, we're a very victim-orientated bunch of people, so they're suffering because people are constantly resisting life as it is. The children learn to

resist life. It is not until they get an understanding that they are creating their own reality that they can do anything about it. You have to see that your resistance to life is creating your suffering and you have to see that you're creating that, that you're 100 per cent responsible for making you feel, that the world doesn't make you feel and can't make you feel. You're responsible, and an immature mind isn't going to really pick that up. They're more likely going to take on the understandings and the beliefs of their peers and growing up in a victim-orientated environment. Well, they're going to suffer. That's how it is.

When a child is born, it is born into suffering until it dies. But there is a possibility, and that possibility is to learn to not resist and to learn to wake up and to learn to serve Heart. These are possibilities that are very, very different. And this is the way of the sannyasin. This is the way of the seeker, to wake up, to die before the body does and be free.

~

S: Is the end of suffering a gradual process, or does it come instantly with awakening?
V: No, it's a gradual process. I learned not to suffer way before awakening. I learned how not to suffer, gosh, when I was 19. I saw that we create our own reality by the way we think, that we're responsible, that we cannot be hurt by the world. We are hurt by ourselves, by our own resistance to life, by our own victim-orientated thinking, that we do it to ourselves. You create your reality. The world is the way the world is. You can accept it or not accept it.

Your choice. You can resist what is or not resist what is. Your choice. You can suffer or not suffer. Your choice. People say "No, it's not my choice". "They did this. This is what happened to me. It's everyone else's problem." Yeah right! You make yourself feel. I don't care what you say, I know this for a fact. You cannot make me feel. That's not possible. Only I can do that. You can do negative things. You may try to harm me. So what! Only I can make myself feel. I'm responsible.

~

S: Do you consider empathy or feeling for people as a form of suffering?

V: No, not a form of suffering, but a form of pain because if you truly are empathising with someone, you're feeling them. You're really feeling them. And if they're in pain, you're feeling the pain too. But if you don't resist the pain, you're not suffering. It doesn't mean you don't feel pain though. You still feel pain. You just don't suffer because you don't resist. The more you open up, the higher in consciousness you go actually, the more sensitive you become, the more you feel. That's how it is, because in lower consciousness, we're all closed down or defended. Trying not to feel, but unfortunately that keeps us locked in lower consciousness. If you really want to raise your consciousness levels, you don't stay defended, you open up. But you do tend to feel more because you're more sensitive. But if you don't resist what you feel, you don't suffer, but you will feel pain.

~

S: If I make you laugh, does that mean I made you feel?

V: No, I made myself laugh, but what you said was funny and you're trying to be tricky. Oh dear. You see, most people do not want to take responsibility for themselves. They want to somehow blame the world or blame someone else or even blame themselves. They want to be a victim, and I'll tell you what, you have to volunteer to be a victim. Bad things can happen to two people. One person decides, oh, it's everyone's fault but mine, and they suffering incredibly in the resistance, and the other takes responsibility and sees this is just what it is and doesn't suffer at all. Choice. You have to choose to be a victim. Choose wisely. You have to choose to suffer because you have to choose to resist life. Pain is not suffering, it is pain. Discomfort is not suffering, it is discomfort. It is the resistance to those that creates suffering and you're in charge of whether you resist or whether you do not. Nobody else. You. You have a look. Examine your own mind. Check this out for yourself. Don't take my word for it. Find out for yourself. Watch yourself, watch your mind. Watch what it does, and watch other people, how they create suffering for themselves. Watch it and you will see and you'll see clearly that we create our own reality by the way we think. Your suffering or your freedom is in your hands. Never volunteer to be a victim. Life is just the way it is. It's up to you.

Thank you for satsang. Good to see you bravehearts here today.

CHAPTER FOUR

What is it like to live as Awareness?

S: Hello Vishrant. Can you please talk about the topic, what is it like to live as awareness?
V: Okay. If you've had satoris, you'll have an understanding to some degree because you'll have some reference points as to what it's like to live as Beingness. If you haven't had satoris, if you've heard about them or studied them, you probably don't have the reference points required.

The mind is what most people think they are and they believe they are the body as a result, but there's something that is purely aware of the mind and it is always here. Rarely do people actually see it. Rarely does awareness become aware of itself. If it does, it's called satori. Someone who's awake is living as that awareness. They're no longer living as an "I" or a body. They're living, or existing – that's a better way of putting it – as awareness, pure awareness, which is what we all are. We are all pure awareness, but there's a belief which is not real that we are the mind and body.

Someone who's awake is simply living as reality, living as pure awareness, and one of the beauties of that is it can't be touched by anything. The mind, on the other hand, the ego on the other hand, can be touched by just about everything, but what we truly are doesn't get touched by anything. It's never born. It cannot die. The quest for the seeker is to find themselves as pure awareness and live as that. That is Enlightenment if it's ongoing. It is quantumly different than living as an ego. In existing as pure awareness, the mind is dropped anyway. It doesn't want to talk to itself. It rests in Beingness. The identification that it has with being a somebody has gone because there's nobody here. You take away your imagination and you take away your ego, because the ego is made up of imagination. It's made up of reference points from the past projected to the future and a few belief systems. You take away your imagination and the ego that you think you are is not here because it's not real. What you are is still here, pure awareness is still here, but it's not personal. The whole quest for freedom, the whole quest for Enlightenment, is to know self as pure awareness or Truth and exist as that that's aware of itself.

So, the games begin. How do you turn awareness back to itself? How do you find yourself as Truth? Find yourself someone who's awake and go and sit with them. Practising self-inquiry, practising meditation, practising openness in the presence of someone who's awake makes it much easier to find yourself as Truth. The energy field of someone who's awake starts to expand the mind, starts to dissolve it to some degree, starts to take you into no-mind. Any meditator who is worth their salt knows no-mind through meditation practice. Yet, even though there's no mind, nobody thinking, no thinking at all, you're still there. What is it that is still there? What is it that is aware of the no-mind? Find that and be free, and then you recognise the illusion of imprisonment and the illusion of freedom because you have always been Beingness, always been pure awareness, pure consciousness.

So how does an awakened person live? Here, always here.

Any questions, any statements, any challenges to this teaching, today?

S: Did you have to be living always here before your awakening?

V: Pretty much. The practice of meditation teaches you to live in the moment rather than in dream. Most human adults live in dream to a large degree, in other words awareness aware of thinking. Someone who's a practised meditator is more present to what is real because the understanding is clear. What you think is not real. Maybe what you see is real. What you hear is real. But what you think is not. Before awakening, present-moment awareness was quite profound because there wasn't much interest in dreaming, there was more of an interest in reality. Meditation, the practice of meditation, teaches you how to witness the mind and teaches you how to see through the mind so you don't get caught in its obstacles. It's very beautiful in that way. Present-moment awareness or the power of now is being present to what is real. The only thing that is not real is what you think.

~

S: Is it useful to have an intellectual understanding that we are pure awareness?
V: Yep. That's good. The intellectual understanding that we're pure awareness can give you the motivation that you require to find the real thing for yourself, to have – rather than an intellectual understanding, a direct knowing – a direct knowing as a result of awareness being aware of itself. Anything that fires up the thirst for Truth is worthy so an intellectual understanding could fire up the thirst for Truth. On the other hand, it could make someone complacent because they might think they already understand it, already know it. Unless you're living as pure awareness, you don't know much, not really. Borrowed knowledge or old knowledge or memory is pretty worthless. It's still dream.

Pure awareness is always here. It is not a dream. When it is aware of itself, it is Enlightenment. It is not a dream, it is not an understanding, it is not a remembering. It is awareness aware of itself in this moment.

~

S: Namaste Vishrantji. How do you know that your Enlightenment is real and not a delusion?
V: The only way that you can tell if someone is awake is by the Buddha field that surrounds them. There is no other way because anyone can say the right words, anyone can have the correct hand gestures, the right mannerisms. If someone is awake, they have a Buddha field and that Buddha field can be felt. It flattens the mind out to some degree and expands the mind

and it is very beautiful to be in. If that Buddha field is not there, the person is not awake. No matter what they say, they are not awake. For someone who is truly enlightened, that Buddha field is there 24 hours a day, seven days a week.

~

S: Can the Buddha field be imagined by the mind or held in memory in a way?

V: Anything can be imagined. People can imagine love, they can imagine silence. They can imagine stillness. They can imagine anything. The mind is wonderful at imagining. Someone might imagine that they're enlightened. They might imagine that their mind is still. They might imagine that they are loving, but energy doesn't lie. Anybody that is loving has a loving energy field. Anybody that's awake has a Buddha field and it can be perceived. If it's not there, they're not awake. Tune in.

~

S: Can you please describe what was happening with your relationships as your consciousness was reaching higher levels?

V: Yeah. One of the beautiful things that happened as a result of consciousness levels rising was obstacles were being removed, belief systems were being undone, defence systems were being undone, and because of that, an enormous amount of love was being perceived because love seems to appear or is perceived more easily in openness, and as a result of that there was a lot of love. At the same time that consciousness levels were rising and awareness was aware of itself, relationships became a little difficult. A great deal of love, but no person. The "I" had dropped so there was nothing really personal, a lot of love, but nothing personal.

So 22 years ago when awakening first occurred, there wasn't a sense of being a human anymore let alone a father or a husband. It had just gone out the window. The ego had dropped. There was this sense of nothing or nobody being here. So relationship was a little difficult, not from the perspective of here, but from the perspective of the other. I remember after a week or two, I recall my wife saying "I have lost my husband" and I couldn't deny it because the one who had been the husband had surrendered unconditionally and there was now an absence of that one. Yet I was still here, but "I" as pure awareness, the big "I", not the little "I". And this is what we all are. We are this big "I". The little "I", the ego, drops. It disappears, and so does its connection with the world to a large degree. I'm here, but I'm not of here. Not really. I'm in this world, but I'm not of it. If you come and sit with me, you'll find the emptiness, you'll find the silence, and you'll find the stillness, because it's here. And what you're starting to perceive is your own true nature, which is pure awareness, and it's always here. Relationships can be a little difficult, though. There is a lot of love. And when love is present, everybody and everything is taken care of.

~

S: Were there any relationships that didn't survive as a result?

V: Most of them. Relationships survive? It's difficult to be with someone who's free because in a lot of ways, they're not here anymore. In a lot of ways, they've gone. The chair is actually empty. There's a lot of love, but there's not much person so it is difficult but possible. All right, all the relationships, all the relationships left except maybe the relationship with my daughters. That's still there, but it's the funniest thing really because the love that is there for them is the same love that is there for everybody else. This idea of personal love is only achieved by a sense of being a somebody, a sense of being an "I", but that is not real, and upon Enlightenment that "I" drops. So this personal "I" drops. There's still love, but there's nobody loving. There's still caring, but there's nobody caring. There's still taking care, but there's nobody taking care. If you've had a satori or two, you understand what I'm talking about. Otherwise, it'll just be intellectual. And you need to find out. What is this that's aware? What is my true nature? This is the question the seeker asks: "Who am I really?"

S: Is care equal to love?

V: No. No, the mind can be caring without love. The mind can be helpful without love. Love is amazing. It's the true jewel of consciousness, and how it affects the mind is very beautiful. But for it to affect the mind, the mind has to be open. It can't be defended. It can't be closed or in resistance to life because all of those things cut off the perception of love.

It's up to you. How open are you? How closed are you? How defended are you? If you're interested in love, open up, drop your defences and wear your heart on your sleeve where it belongs. And yeah, you'll probably get hurt, but that's the price for loving. That's the price for perceiving love. All of our defence systems that stop us from getting hurt are absolutely obstacles in the way of love. They create us as separate.

~

S: As your Buddha field affects the other person, who's driving the car?
V: Yes. I'm very, very careful with whom I let drive me anywhere because some people get very ungrounded in the energy field, and ungrounded people behind the wheel of a car are dangerous. And so yes, the people in the car get affected, the driver included, and so I'm careful. I remember I was doing satsangs down south for a while, 160km, and I had a woman drive me and I started to notice how ungrounded she was getting and it was time to change drivers. I remember when I sat with Osho Rajneesh back in the 80s, I used to get so out there, it was like I was walking on air.

This is what happens around someone who's got a Buddha field: you get ungrounded. I have problems with cashiers. I go to pay and they count the money over and over again because they keep losing their minds. This is what happens. It's just how it is. The Buddha field is very beautiful, but it definitely can affect people quite strongly.

~

S: Are there any outer obstacles to higher consciousness such as anger directed towards you in response to boundaries placed?

V: Only if you react otherwise. No.

What happens outside of you is irrelevant. It's your reaction to what happens outside of you that is relevant to you. If there is no reaction, perfect. If there's a reaction of contraction, constriction, defensiveness, well, you've taken yourself into lower consciousness. It's all about how you react or how you do not react, and usually that's related to how conscious you are and what belief systems you're running – what kind of expectations you have on those belief systems.

The work that needs to be done to support Enlightenment is the work of the mind to make itself equanimous so it doesn't react by contracting and going down the chute, so it stays open, which is a non-reaction. This is very beautiful, to have a mind that is non-reactive, but that's up to you. Only you can create that because you're responsible 100 per cent for your reactions.

~

S: Hi Vishrant. I wanted to make a couple of comments about the Buddha field and ask about relationships.

I know they have measured brainwaves so I'm not at all sceptical that it's a thing, but it seems to have been affecting my wife quite a bit. We were driving home yesterday and I said Vishrant claims the Buddha field can go up to a kilometre, which I am pretty sceptical about. She goes "Oh no, I'm sure it can". At one point I said no. I saw recently that as people become more aware of awareness or even are in the presence of a Buddha field a lot, it can be very scary for them because it highlights that who we think we are doesn't have the solidity in reality that we think. I said to her that I think it can even be scary and she really jumped on that and said "Yes, it can be scary". I guess it's unsettling and anything unsettling can be scary. Our relationship is still good. She actually had some health problems and when they turned out to be solid and good, she felt a lot better. I've even heard people can almost feel like they're dying when they get close to Enlightenment because the ego is dying. So I'm wondering about two things: how my capacity to function will change – you've talked about that – and also how my ability to relate to people will change. But you seem very normal and we've had many conversations so I'm a little bit surprised to hear that you lost all of these friends, and why would that be? That really surprised me that you said that.

V: For the first six months after awakening, I sat still in a chair 18 hours a day and stared into space because there was nothing inside of me that was moving. My mind was resting in Beingness, blissed out. It wasn't until one of my Advaita Vedanta teachers came along and said, "Look, you've got to come out of here and start being in the world" that I came out. Then I had to learn to be human again. My mind wasn't working. It was silent, and so socially I was inept. I didn't even blink. I had to learn to look away when I talked to people. I had to learn to blink. I had to learn to behave like a human again because I was so gone. So you're meeting me today, 22 years later, where I've had a lot of practice pretending to be a human because Beingness is not human.

S: So that's a concern to me, because I don't know how to gauge how close I am. I certainly spent a lot of hours just in Truth, and it's true, I can't function well. If I were to let go of these final fears, you know, I have this notion that I have to worry about things and I'm starting to realise that just isn't true.

V: If you're willing – if you're willing to surrender everything – you can be free. Anything you try holding on to – and fear is all about holding on – will keep you away from Enlightenment. The hardest thing for me to actually surrender and give up really was my children, but I had to, so I did. Not that I ever went away from them. That never occurred. But the attachment to them had to be dropped. When we look at attachment, it's all future-orientated anyway, it's about what we want for the future, or what we're hanging on to for the future. That has to be dropped as well because that's not real either. The future is not real. Attachments are imprisonments that keep us suffering. To truly be free we need to let go of everything, but we don't have to physically leave. It's like some things left and some things stayed. Some things came back after they left, but there was such freedom in not hanging on to anything.

S: Okay. Thank you.

V: You've got to look at what hangs on. What's hanging on? It's the ego. It's the "I" that's hanging on. Of course, while it's hanging on, awareness stays on the "I". You may be flip-flopping. In other words, awareness may be going to itself from time to time and then back to the ego that's hanging on you. If you really want to be free, you've got to let go. No future.

S: Well it almost makes me wonder if I need to plan for being non-functional for months. I mean, I have no idea how close I am. So there's that.

V: You've got to be okay with everything failing. If you can be okay with everything failing, you can be free.

S: Okay. There's almost a chemical juice from the addiction to worry and then the second part is there's a belief that it's necessary and useful and it's just not.

V: Well it is good for survival, but awakening is not about survival. The ego is all about survival. What we are, pure awareness, doesn't need to survive because it was never born and it cannot die. Survival belongs to the mind. If the mind is willing to let go, if it's willing to die, you can know yourself as Truth instead of this thing that wants to survive.

S: Yeah. And the whole long story and everything I've been through is not going to be me anymore if I cross the line.

V: That's true. Be here now and this is all that's real. Nothing else is real. Everything else is imagined outside this moment.

Is there anything else?

S: No. Thanks for everything.
V: Good to talk to you.

~

S: Can you speak on the unconscious mind and if you think using it as a tool is good?
V: Usually you're not conscious of it because it is unconscious. In developing a silent witness that witnesses the mind through the practice of meditation, you start to see deeper and deeper and deeper layers of the mind so what is subconscious, what is unconscious, gets to be exposed. You start seeing the nuts and the bolts of how the mind works. You see all of its hidden agendas, all of its belief systems, all of its defence systems, all of its lies, and now that you can see it, you can do something about it. What can be done is undoing it so it is no longer in the way. Satsang is really a process of undoing, not a process of building up or becoming bigger, better and more powerful. That's personal growth. Satsang is an unlearning process so you can be free.

~

S: What is the Buddha field?
V: The best way to find out is to find someone who's awake and go and sit with them and then get as close as you can to them and become silent inside yourself so you can perceive the energy that is in the room. The energy that is in the room is called a Buddha field and it is produced when awareness is aware of itself inside a human being. In other words, when you're sitting with someone who's enlightened, they have an energy field.

In Christianity, they say the saints have halos. Well, that halo is a little bit like a Buddha field. Someone who's awake has a Buddha field, a field of energy that can be perceived by those who are sensitive. This energy field has the ability to expand the mind, expand the Heart, and take you into reality. The best way to find out is go sit with someone who's awake and get as close as you can and if you can engage them in conversation, engage them in conversation because when you're talking directly to someone who's awake, the field of energy is stronger.

~

S: Does satori produce a temporary Buddha field?
V: Yes. Some satsang teachers actually can sit for an hour and self-inquire and find themselves in Beingness as Beingness and then hold satsang, but these people aren't fully awake, they're half-baked enlightened. They're flip floppers. They're going from ego-based reality to Being-based reality and then back again. There's something in them that is not completely surrendered. There's something in them that's not complete yet. So someone having a satori, while that satori is occurring, will have a Buddha field, yes.

~

S: If someone had a satori, would it be obvious to the person having it?
V: No, not necessarily, because the satoris range from very, very small, to very, very big. You can suddenly find yourself as stillness and silence, it's a small satori, very small, or you could find yourself as the

universe and every particle in it, very big, or you could find yourself as absolutely nothingness, big. The best way to find out is to self-inquire, asking the question, "Who's aware?" Or "What's aware?" See if you can't turn awareness back to itself and get a glimpse, or in deep meditation, same. Practice is what works. We're very practised at living as an ego. Practise finding what is aware of the ego. What's aware of the mind? What's aware of the thoughts? Practise that.

~

S: Is reiki similar to being close to a Buddha field?
V: No, it's an energy field that's produced, but it's not the same. It's not similar at all, no.

~

S: You were speaking about being ungrounded in the Buddha field. What do you mean by ungrounded and is it possible to not get ungrounded in the Buddha field?
V: Yes it is. People can be grounded in different forms of reality. We can be grounded in our minds, which is not a good place to be grounded because it's unstable. We can be grounded in our bodies which are much more stable because they're more real. So when we have awareness locked in our body, and if you shake hands with an athlete or someone who works physically with their hands, you'll find that their energy field is in their hands, it's in their body. And these people are grounded in their body. Most people tend to be grounded more in their minds. If you're grounded in your mind, when you come into

the presence of someone who's awake and the mind starts expanding, you will lose your grounding. You become ungrounded. If you're grounded in your body, it's easier because awareness is still with what's real, the body. For someone who's ungrounded, we're usually referring to someone who's actually not functioning well in the mind because they're not in touch with reality in any source, at any source. They're not in touch with the body. They're not in touch with Beingness, they're just gone. Being ungrounded is not good. If you're driving a car, it's not good. If you're riding a pushbike, it's not good, or if you're trying to have a conversation with someone.

It's best to be grounded, so one of the things that I got into was walking – what I called Walking in Zen. That's where you walk and you put your awareness in your body, you put your awareness in your footfalls, you put awareness in your breath. And you put awareness all around you as well, like in the sounds around you, the wind, the sun on you, and the sound, the everything around you. And in that way, you're not putting awareness on thoughts because you have awareness on everything else. You can't think. Now if you're walking in Zen, you've got your awareness in your body because you've got your awareness on your foot falls, so you're practising keeping awareness in the body, and you become very grounded in the body rather than grounded in the mind. And being grounded in the body, rather than grounded in the mind, is a lot easier in the world in a lot of ways because you're not caught in dream. You're being real. You're not caught in imaginings, in thoughts, you're just here. Now, this is not necessary. This is not awake. But it's aware of what is real rather than what is not. And so meditation, walking, walking meditation, even sitting meditation, allows you to be aware of what is real. Unfortunately, most people think what they think is real, but there's nothing real about what you think. It's imagined. Look around you and what you see is real. What you hear is real. Maybe what you feel is real, but what you think about it is not. And so being grounded in the body allows you to have a more realistic life before awakening.

~

S: Can you talk more about being grounded and the importance of that for Enlightenment?

V: I don't know if it's important for Enlightenment. I was very, very into being grounded in my body for 20 years before awakening occurred. I loved reality. I loved being present to what is real. I didn't have much time for dreaming because I saw it as a place where people suffered in their minds, imagining all sorts of things that were real that were not. My whole adventure in this lifetime has been very much of one who's been present in reality. I loved diving. I loved racing cars. I loved racing motorbikes. I loved sport. I loved martial arts. I loved anything that took me into my body and out of my head, and I think that because of that it was actually an aid to awareness being aware of itself because I was used to being with what is real and I had no interest in what I was thinking. I'd already to some degree surrendered the thinking mind. It was being used as a tool rather than just as a constant chatter, chatter, chatter, chatter. I love to see the nature. I love to feel my footfalls. I love to feel my body. I love to dance, actually, because you're in your body. Unfortunately, we all go to school and we learn how to live in our heads. We didn't live there before we went to school, we were actually in reality to a large degree before we went to school, and we went to school and we learnt to live in our heads so we could remember things and pass examinations. Most adults never leave that. They remain living in their heads as problem solvers until the day they die rather than getting back into reality which is at a basic level the body and at an ultimate level awareness aware of itself. That is the ultimate reality. That is who we are.

~

S: I've been hearing about the progressive path and direct path and self-inquiry. Can they be practised simultaneously or not?

V: I would need to have you explain what direct path and progressive path is because I'm not familiar with it. My understanding of self-inquiry is really, really simple. You inquire "Who's aware?" and find the witness as yourself. I'm not sure what progressive path is. You'd have to explain it to me. It sounds like some teacher has set up some kind of way of teaching that is his style or her style that I'm not familiar with.

~

S: Isn't putting awareness on real things kind of opposite from the goal of awareness on nothingness?

V: In a way, but its way better to have awareness on real things than having awareness on a dream that is not real and everything you think is not real. And because of the way we've been programmed, more than likely what you're putting awareness on is a problem-solving machine that worries and gets upset. Wouldn't it be better to have awareness on what is real, and then turn awareness back to what is ultimately real, our own true self? So if you were to meet me personally, and you shook my hand, which I don't do much anymore, but if you did, you'd find that the awareness is actually in the body. It's not just on itself. Awareness is in the body. It's also on itself. And because of that, I can be in the world quite strongly. If awareness was just on itself, it would be difficult to be in the world.

~

S: Is every satori different? The mind tends to remember the last one and hold on to it or look for the same experience. Should that be avoided?

V: It's going in and coming out of satori that is different. Satori itself? We are nothing, there's nothing, there's absolutely nothing here and there's everything here. This can't be understood. It can only be known directly. But it is always the same – the same as someone who's awake has a Buddha field and that Buddha field will be the same as anybody else who's awake because Beingness is like the ocean. No matter what part of the ocean you go to, it's still salty, it's the same. So don't worry about changes, don't worry about differences. Just keep looking for self as Truth. Self-inquire until there is no one left to inquire.

~

S: What is the difference, if any, between the ultimate reality or Truth that teachers speak about, and pure awareness?

V: None. Same. As a matter of fact, everything is Truth. Everything, everything is God. It's just that most people aren't aware of that. They're aware of their mind, and through the mind their senses, and so they miss the big picture. The big picture is we are . . . we are this, we are everything. This is the big picture. The small picture is "I am a somebody" which is actually not even real. Yet truthfully, we are that too. But we're also everywhere else. Beingness is everything. It's not separate from anything. There is no separation in Beingness. There is only one.

~

S: What was it about the nature of awareness that was attractive to you?

V: You heard about curiosity killing the cat? I found that I was very curious as to what was at the top of the mountain. Once I climbed the mountain and found what was at the top, my mind fell in love with it, decided to die for it.

~

S: How long do you have to practise being aware of awareness before it comes naturally to you?

V: Before it becomes a default pattern, stuck on, like, awareness gets locked onto itself like two permanent magnets? Honestly, I don't know. I have no idea why that actually happened for me. I have no idea really. It just happened. One day, I found myself as pure awareness without anybody here 21 years ago and it's just been like that for 21 years. You could say that a lot of work was done to produce a mind that would support that, but I think there's more involved in that. I think there's something to do with karma. Sometimes gurus refer to it as grace, but I think its karma.

~

S: When you were a psychotherapist and you were crying with your clients, did you find that you cried less as belief systems were uninstalled?

~

V: It wasn't so much the belief systems being uninstalled that stopped the crying. What stopped the crying was the end of the pain body that was being released, the end of the sadness that was inside of me being released. I had, like most other human adults, a pain body that I'd carried from lifetime to lifetime, and as they were emptied as a result of allowing myself to fully feel them, there was just nothing left after a while. Not much to do with belief systems, more to do with a willingness to actually feel.

~

S: Your bhakti path of service to and love of others, is this a response to your egoic past as a highly competitive person? Would your expression of Truth be different if you came to being this as a less dynamic personality?

V: Look, the reason I am the way I am in the world is totally resultant from love being perceived. When love is perceived by the mind, it just wants to take care of everyone and everything. This is how love affects the mind. It's very beautiful. And so that's it. That's the bottom line. It's love, nothing else, not because of this path or that path, but simply because there's enough openness for love to be perceived pretty much constantly while I'm out here. As a result of that there's this attitude of "What can I do for you? How can I help you? How can I lift you?" And it's beautiful.

~

S: Sometimes I feel that the dream of the future is what is making me want to live in this world. Why would this be the case?

V: That's because the now is awful. Look, if you really open your eyes and you have a look around, you'll notice that just about everyone is suffering one way or another or they're finding a way to escape their suffering. Whether it's alcohol, food, do-aholism, everybody's trying to get away from their pain. When you really open your eyes and you have a look at the world, and you have a look at yourself, you see that everyone's suffering. It's tragic. It's best to get free. It's best to get out of the dream that keeps you away from the suffering that's here because the dream's not real. While you're dreaming, you're not living – you're existing in a dream that's not real. You're wasting this beautiful life. Stop dreaming and be with what's real. You will have to deal with what's inside of you and you will see what's actually happening around you. The dreams or the future projections that we live in can keep us away from a lot of things. Hope is the great enemy of Enlightenment, same as fear is, because they're both future projections that have nothing to do with reality. They keep us locked in a dream. Quite often if you go to a Buddhist temple, you will notice above the door, "Abandon hope". Abandon all hope because hope is seen for what it is: a dream. It's actually in the way of being present to the moment, present to what is real. Have a look for yourself and see. Abandon all hope, abandon all fear. What is real?

~

S: Can you speak on life's problems such as poverty and pain not being able to last long once enlightened?

V: I'm not sure actually what you're asking me because if you're living in the moment and you're not living in your head, there are no problems. The only problem comes in when there's an "I" present. And if there's no "I", there are no problems. It's just what is in the moment. You can stay cool because you're not dreaming, but I'm not sure what you're asking me there. It's not very clear to me. It's not like, you wake up and you don't feel pain. You still feel pain, but you're not resisting it anymore. You don't have a story about you anymore. It's just what is. The same as there might be bliss. It's just what is.

~

S: Now coming to the present moment fully and letting go of constant thinking, I often find myself not feeling very nice. Why is this?

V: More than likely, you've been using some form of escape by doing or moving or dreaming to avoid what's inside of you. And when you stop doing those escape methodologies, what's inside of you starts to surface and it's unpleasant, it feels unpleasant. This is what I refer to as wounding, what Jung referred to as the dark night of the soul, and all seekers have to go through it to get free. You have to empty the house. I love the analogy of the house being full and no room for God to live in the house, the house being the body, the vehicle. Empty the house. Empty the house and become sattvic so God can live here. It's only an analogy, but in a way it's true. Emptying the house means no more problems.

~

S: If I wake up feeling crappy, am I emptying the house?
V: Maybe. Sounds like it. Sounds like you're purging. Something deep down is coming up that's making you feel bad. Either that or you're ill. Quite often when we go to sleep at night, we let off a lot of density from the day. We let off a lot of pain body because we're not holding it down in any way, and if we have been doing that, we could wake up feeling murky, we could wake up feeling not so good. It's best to clear the house. It's best to become sattvic.

~

S: I've listened to motivational speakers in the past. Do you recommend building dreams to achieve goals? Is there a problem with this do you think?
V: Heck yeah. I've listened to motivational teachers in the past as well. I used to actually be one. I used to train salespeople how to sell. It's all about creating goals and dreams. It never stops. It never stops. It's

just another form of discontentment. Find yourself as pure awareness and be free. If you really want to have goals, have goals, but don't put too much energy into thinking about it. All thinking is dreaming. All dreaming is in the way of reality. And really, when we look at setting goals, if we want to set a goal, it only takes a short period of time. Then when it comes time, we execute the plan to get the goal. We don't need to constantly live in our heads, rambling over it, procrastinating. How about just being free? How about being in the moment and spending as much of your time with reality as you can rather than with dream which is never really satisfying. You watch the mind for a while. It desires things to be different constantly. There's no satisfaction in that. It gets attached to things that it thinks it owns and then gets frightened of losing them. There is no joy in that. That's dissatisfaction as well. Get present. It's nice. It's beautiful just to be here, and when you were a little kid, probably under the age of four or five, you were just here. You didn't live in your head yet. The practice of meditation, the practice of mindfulness is really the practice of getting real, reclaiming reality from a dream that you've been lost in. But it's up to you because whatever you practise, you're going to get good at. If all you practise is thinking, well, that's all you're going to be good at. How about practising being with what is real? And ultimately, what is real is pure awareness.

Thank you for satsang. Good to see you bravehearts here today.

CHAPTER FIVE

The Price for Enlightenment

V: Welcome to Satsang.
S: Hello Vishrant, can you please talk about the topic, the price for Enlightenment?
V: Price for Enlightenment?

Well, there is no real price to be who you are. We are all Beingness we are all Truth. We're all everything. It's just that some people aren't aware of that and because they're not aware of that, they want it. They hunger for it. They seek it out. They search for it. They try to get it and they miss it so they go to find themselves or they read a book on the subject or they find themselves a guru who's talking about the subject and they get interested. Then at some point they realise that awareness is what we truly are because all teachers teach that we are just pure consciousness, pure awareness, and they get an intellectual understanding that we are pure awareness. Then the quest begins. Well, how do we discover that we are pure awareness and that pure awareness is always here, it's just not aware of itself?

There's a certain problem in that. The seeker starts looking and finds that the thing that's in the way is the constant dreaming. When we have a look at what's actually dreaming, it's the mind, it's the "I", and we get an understanding that the obstacle that's in the way of awareness being aware of itself and staying aware of itself is that awareness is locked on to this dreaming, this identification of being a somebody which is based on reference points, which are also a dream. So the price, if there is such a thing as a price, is the removal of the obstacles that are in the way of awareness being aware of itself.

These obstacles show up as basically anything that contracts us, anything that takes us into lower consciousness, anything that takes us into dream, really. If you go to a monastery or an ashram, they'll teach you how to meditate. They'll teach you how to reclaim reality. Being in meditation is being aware of what's real, so reclaim reality from the dream that you are lost in. But people believe their dream to be real. They think they are somebody, they think they have a future, they think they have a past, but this is all thoughts, not reality. There's something that's aware of all of this and it's that that's aware that we're looking for. It's that that's aware that awareness needs to become aware of for Enlightenment to occur. So the price is, you remove everything that's in the way. The mind actually dedicates itself to reality, to Truth instead of to itself. The mind in most human beings is dedicated to itself, is dedicated to its survival and dedicated to its future, dedicated to a whole pile of dreams that aren't real. But as long as we're dedicated to dreams, well, we're going to live as dreams because that's where our awareness is going to be. We always live where awareness is focused so if our awareness is on our dreams, our mind, we live as that. If awareness is on awareness, we live as Beingness, we live as Truth.

That's the potential for all human beings. The only reason I can see in being here is to wake up to our true nature, but the mind doesn't want to give anything up for it, not really. It wants that and it wants to keep everything it's got. It wants to keep all of its dreams, wants to keep everything it's attached to, and that doesn't actually work. As long as it's holding on to things, awareness is going to be locked on to it and not on itself. So the price is everything. You can have everything in the world you want, but you can't be attached to it.

Attachment keeps us locked in lower consciousness so the Buddha had his monks and nuns become celibate, put on saffron robes, have a begging bowl and become beggars. They may have had sandals, but they didn't have a great deal. He was taking all of the things they may get attached to away from them and that works to some degree, but the truth is, if we're not attached to things, we can have anything and be free. It's our attachment that causes the problems. You could say the price is letting go of our attachments so awareness can find itself and stay on itself without coming back to something or contracting because we're frightened of losing something. Those who are getting close to awakening get to a point where they realise that, well, you can serve your mind or you can serve Truth, but you can't really serve both. Those who wake up serve reality and in the service of reality, in the service of Truth, the mind stays stable because it doesn't attract attention back to itself.

What is it that you don't want to give up for Truth? What is it that you want to hang on to? Have a look at what is it you're attached to and you'll see what's in the way and there's nothing wrong, I will say it again, there's nothing wrong with having things, having relationships, having children, having businesses, having objects or property. It's the attachment to them that is the problem. Let go, let go, let go – and be free. Have a look at what you serve. That's not a bad idea. Have a look. What do you actually serve, keeping in mind that those who are free serve Truth?

S: Some days I feel a bursting desire to give up everything for Truth, and some days I get lost in the mundane again. What could help me to not lose track of the goal ever again?

V: Waking up helps you not lose track of the goal ever again. I was talking about service before, and the service from the mind's perspective is, what does the mind serve? But the truth is, we're not the mind, we're not the body. It's just that if the mind is trying to serve Truth, it will serve Truth. If it is not trying to serve Truth, it'll probably serve itself. If you want to wake up, turn awareness on awareness and have the mind fall in love with that and then it will serve that. Find Beingness, find pure awareness itself, even just in satori, and fall in love with that and give that your totality because it's a love affair that occurs between the mind and Truth that allows the mind to surrender unconditionally. It's in that love affair that the mind is willing to die for Truth, really.

You can come and sit in the presence of someone who's awake, which is what I did, and after a while I fell in love with the presence, I fell in love with the beauty. Eventually I realised what I'd fallen in love with wasn't a man or a woman sitting holding satsang. It was Beingness. I'd fallen, my mind had fallen in love with Beingness, and in that love affair it learned to surrender. In that love affair it died. Unconditional surrender is a death. It's the death of the "I". And then awareness can stay on itself. Beingness can then stay on itself quite easily. Then there is no two anymore. There's no you and me anymore. There's just one, just one, just here, different aspects of the one.

Keep turning awareness back to itself and fall in love from the mind's perspective. Fall in love with Truth and then you'll do whatever it takes.

~

S: I had an experience a few days ago where I really realised or at least took myself to be Beingness, almost looking down at whatever it is I take myself to be most of the time, and I'm sort of looking into the abyss, one way you put it the other day. Is there really nothing I can do to experience myself as Beingness more because it certainly feels like a much healthier, definitely more pleasant state?

V: You can, as I understand your question. Look at the helper thoughts, the ones that try to advise you, the ones that try to let you know what's happening, how deep you've gone or how gone you are – how any thought, any thought that comes from the mind to support awakening will be an obstacle to awakening because awareness will go back to the thoughts.

So don't touch the mind. Really don't touch the mind. Let it go. If it rambles on just witness it, but don't get involved in it.

S: So it really can't help me to be the awareness?

V: It can ask the question, "Who's aware?" But the moment it starts measuring, the moment it starts thinking that it can help, it's in the way. And that's how the ego survives, by becoming helper thoughts.

S: So even this question is, in some sense, in the way?

V: Yeah. Just when awakening was starting to occur here, I noticed the helper thoughts, measuring, even the self-inquiry to some degree, and I saw quite clearly they were also in the way, that really no-mind is best. So I just didn't entertain the mind. If the mind came up, I just didn't entertain it. I witnessed it, but I didn't entertain it because I could see that in entertaining it, awareness goes back to the mind.

S: Yeah that makes a lot of sense.

V: In the early stages of Enlightenment, from my perspective, the fragile situation, awareness can flip-flop back and forth quite easily from itself to back to the mind, to back to itself, back to the mind, and the best the mind can do is be quiet. Then awareness locks onto itself and it can't come off. It just locks on, but that takes a certain amount of time or practice. I don't really understand the whole process. I just saw it happening that one day it was so locked on there was no way it was going to come off, no matter what happened. It was just locked on. But in the early stages, it was fragile. It could quite easily have slipped back.

S: And how long did it take to get there? Was it a year after you found awareness, that second time, after the 11 years, that it locked on?

V: A year, but what was happening was there were satoris every day. There was probably a couple thousand satoris in that year and there was this recognition that there was something bringing awareness back to the mind, and it was the mind talking to itself. It was trying to help, but it was in the way, it was actually in the way, so I stopped entertaining all thought. Don't touch the mind at all. Don't touch the mind. And let awareness lock onto itself.

S: I really appreciate you. I stumbled on you at just the right time about three months ago. Thanks for everything.

V: Happy to help.

~

S: How can self-hypnosis remove obstacles to awakening? Can you talk about your inner child self-hypnosis method?

V: Yeah, okay. I got into the inner child work a long, long time ago in the 80s, even before it became popular, after recognising that a lot of the damage that was inside of me was represented by images of children who were at that age when the damage occurred. I started going back in my mind to those places as an adult. I'd go and visit that child and actually tell that child that I was there for him and he would never need to be alone again. He would never need to deal with this stuff again because I was there for it. And something melted in me with this. When the child that was representing whatever trauma it was felt supported and nurtured and not alone, it started to relax, and in the relaxation the trauma started to heal. And the thing about that is if we have a very traumatised psyche, we're going to react strongly to the world from time to time, and if we are starting to wake up, awareness is going to go back to the trauma, it's going to go back to the contraction, so it's really good to heal the wounds of our Heart. It's really good to heal trauma. Doing self-hypnosis and going back to the different stages in life where we were traumatised in some way or another as an adult and supporting that inner child definitely helped. For me, it definitely allowed my mind to heal and relax, to open up and relax, so I do recommend it to people if they are interested in healing the wounds of the Heart to do the inner child work.

~

S: Namaste Vishrant. For awareness to lock on to itself permanently, does it require grace?

V: Yes, I would say that's true. Anytime you hear me saying the word "grace", what I'm really saying is "I don't know". Things by grace? Yes, I don't know. That's a better way of putting it. You can do everything right, you can heal the wounds of your Heart, you can slow the mind right down, you can be in meditation all of the time – which means present to reality all of the time – you can be self-inquiring and you can still not wake up because there is another ingredient and that is karma. And you don't know. You just don't know. You don't know how good your karma is or how bad it is. You just have to be willing to accept whatever it is. In that willingness, to accept whatever it is, the mind relaxes and puts itself in a better position for Enlightenment. It is in a relaxed, open, vulnerable state of the mind that unconditional surrender happens and that Enlightenment happens. It's all about being relaxed, from the mind's perspective.

~

S: Dear Vishrant, I've been meditating a lot these past five years, and as a result I have become very blissful almost all of the time, which has no cause. Despite feeling bliss a lot of the time, I know this is not awakening or at least not full awakening. There is definitely a self still left in me, but there also feels like there is nothing more I can do except to remain aware of awareness for full awakening, which brings up a huge fear of death. Did you pass through this fear of death yourself? And did you also feel like there was nothing you could do? I'd love to hear your experience and how you passed through this stage on your path. I have so much gratitude for all your help. Much love to you.

V: Okay, first of all, yes, if you meditate, you will find bliss and people quite often settle for bliss because it's a nice experience.

If we're looking to find who we truly are, we need to discover what's aware of the bliss. It is lovely to have bliss, but what does this bliss appear in? What is the background? What is aware of it? As far as the fear of death is concerned, yeah, well, if you're starting to wake up, the "I" is gonna die and it knows it so it can throw up terror. Fear is its main survival mechanism so unconsciously it'll throw out fear to survive and you've got to go, "Okay, I'll die". Okay. You've got to make it okay. I was fortunate in some ways because I started practising this when I was very young. I was a martial artist and as a martial artist I needed to be okay with death and mutilation because I was doing full-contact martial arts and that was always a possibility. If you're frightened of that, the fear itself has already defeated you before you step into the ring, so I was making it okay to die at a very young age.

When it came to looking at the abyss and the mind realising, well, this is it, it's all over, I'm gonna die. Of course, it doesn't think that, but that's the feeling, and terror arises. I just had to be okay with the terror and the dying. Just make it all okay. In the okayness, something drops. So if terror arises, don't fight it, just make it okay. Fear arises, don't fight it, just make it okay. Okayness is the antidote to everything.

It's up to you. Don't get caught in bliss. Find out what's aware of it. Ask the question "What's aware?" Keep going, keep going, keep going until there's nothing left.

~

S: Hello Vishrant. How do you know when you have found who you truly are?
V: There's nobody there. See, people think they're gonna find something and that's the tricky bit. What happens is there's more of an absence than anything

else because when awareness is aware of itself, the mind has dropped the ego's job, so there's an absence of the somebody. There's more of a noticing of the absence more than anything else. There's just nobody here. There's talking, but there's nobody talking. You see, we have this sense of a somebody being here because we're thinking, we're thinking about the future, we're thinking about the past, we're analysing, but that all drops, and there's nothing here. Just pure awareness. And that is profoundly different than being ego-based, so it can't really be missed.

~

S: I've been inserting doubt into the belief system beneath resentment, but the emotion is persistent. What else can I do?

V: I wonder what the emotion is. Is it anger or is it sadness? I wonder. Just make it okay. Whatever is there, make it okay because if it's repressed emotionality, it probably needs to leave the body, and in making it okay it will leave. In actually warmly welcoming it, it will leave. You may have undone the belief systems, but the load that was created while they were in play, the pain body, may still be there. So now just make it okay for you to feel whatever's there. Be okay with what is, warmly welcome it, let it go, like an old friend that's leaving. It's okay. Nothing to do really. Just make it okay.

S: The emotion is anger.

V: Ah, so anger is a defence system. So that's a little bit different. That's a little bit more difficult to deal with because underneath the anger, there'll be something else. There'll be a hurt and the anger is stopping you from feeling the hurt.

In anger, we feel empowered. In the hurt, we feel disempowered and helpless and quite often hopeless. So anger defends us from feeling that. It's a defence system and it keeps us contracted, and one more thing: anger usually demands a story of some kind. We have to be a victim to be angry. We have to be blaming something or someone or ourselves. But we have to be blaming, otherwise anger doesn't have a great deal of power. It's powered, it's fuelled, by blame. Have a look. Are you still blaming somewhere? If not, and there's just anger, there's just anger, just the feeling of anger, just let it be there. Be okay with it. It's something that's leaving. It's okay, but be aware that it is a defence system and there may be something under it.

~

S: I came across a guy on social media who's not really famous, but in my opinion, a phenomenal artist. I see myself constantly thinking about him, fantasising about who I think he is and how perfect he is. When I meditate regularly, the thoughts about him become less and less, but I still have this deep desire to one day be noticed by him. I really want to learn how to live without forming mental fantasies, the need for approval and recognition from the opposite sex. How do I do this?

V: You always begin with acceptance. You begin with accepting that's how you are. You begin by accepting the patterning and the programming that's there.

This pattern in programming is doing what it's doing and you're witnessing it. But always begin with acceptance. Always. And then watch it. Just witness it. Just witness how it works. Witness what it does, witness its agendas, witness its stories, witness its belief systems. Be the witness of the mind from a place of absolute acceptance and from that place, your mind will show itself in its totality to you. When we truly see what's going on inside our own minds, we have raised our consciousness levels and because we've raised our consciousness levels, we don't need to get caught in some things anymore because we can see clearly that we're banging our head on the wall. We stop because we can see. But it begins with okayness of what it is, and then if we just witness, just watch, just watch and see how it all works, this is brilliant.

~

S: Was the quietening of your mind a slow, gradual process or was it a result of perceiving Beingness?

V: Okay. My mind wasn't that busy before awakening because I wasn't really into entertaining drama. I like reality. I was a meditator and I enjoyed reality more than I enjoyed thinking so it wasn't so hard. When awakening occurred, the mind spoke to itself for probably another six months. In the beginning it was like it was in the room talking and you could hear it. After a week or so it was in another room, further away. You could hear it, but there's no attention being paid to it. After another week, it was further away again, in another room further away. Even though it probably took six months to quieten right down to nothing, it was going further and further away as the detachment from it was greater and greater and greater. And there wasn't an interest. The mind itself wasn't interested in itself. It was interested in Beingness. It was in adoration of Beingness, in service to Beingness. And in service to Beingness, it was being as quiet as it could because it was absolutely in love with Beingness, the beloved.

So it did take a while. It took a while, but as a meditator it had already shut up to a fair extent. Reality's brilliant. Dreaming is not brilliant. It actually just causes suffering usually. The more you can get into reality the better. Meditation simply means being aware of what's real. The only thing that's not real is what you think. It's up to you.

~

S: When my awareness is locked onto itself and there is just Beingness, there is just freedom and contentment. You say that is Enlightenment? Is it that simple? Sometimes when a satori is experienced, I just laugh and say, is it that simple?

V: Well, Enlightenment is when awareness is locked onto itself, 24 hours a day, seven days a week. Satori is when it locks on for a bit and then you go back to ego-based reality. That's satori. It's like a glimpse, a glimpse of the Truth, and anyone can have a glimpse of the Truth at any time because we are the Truth. It's not somewhere else. But Enlightenment is a continuation of that satori. Someone who's enlightened is in satori 24 hours a day, seven days a week. It's not held in memory. Memory is dream. Memory is lower consciousness again. You have a satori and you remember it, you're just dreaming. Someone who's awake is in satori 24 hours a day, seven days a week.

~

S: You mentioned it is okay to have things while pursuing Truth if we are not attached. Many teachers say sex is unique and should be avoided. Is this always true, usually true or what?

V: Not in my experience. It's just another thing that people get attached to. It's a primal program for the reproduction of the species. It's a survival mechanism and we're primally programmed to be attached to it, but like everything else it can be accepted and let go. I'm not against sex. I'm not for sex. Sex is natural. It's okay. Just don't get attached to it. It's the same as anything else. Just don't get attached. Do your best to stay free because if we're really attached to something, if we addictively demand that we have it, we create such a contraction inside our own psyche that even if we are in satori, awareness would go back to the ego that's contracting, that wants what it wants, and is addictively demanding it. Everything, everything has to be accepted, the good, the bad, and the ugly. In that acceptance we can rest, the mind can rest, and having a restful mind is the optimum for higher consciousness and the optimum for enlightenment.

~

S: I've become aware of my thoughts. Now I think it has become a bit difficult to transcend them because I'm constantly checking if I'm okay or if my thoughts are there. How to achieve no-mind?

V: Yeah, yeah, well, just checking is going into thought. How about just watching the breath and walking. I used to do a lot of walking and I'd watch my footfalls. That's where my feet were hitting the ground, I'd be aware of that. I'd be aware of my breath at my nose as I was walking so I was aware of two things: my footfalls and my breath. Then I'd become aware of what I could see and what I could smell and what I could feel, whether the wind was on my face, whether the sun was on my face. And when I became aware of all of these things at once, I couldn't think, because if I had thought, my mind would leave some of these things. So I used to walk and be aware of these things. I called it Walking in Zen. I loved it. I love walking, particularly on beaches, walking in Zen, just being aware of the footfalls, the breath, the sound of the surf, seagulls, the wind on my face, the sun on my shoulder. There was no room for thought. I just was in the moment. It was beautiful.

Just put your awareness on what is real, and put your awareness on a few things that are real and there is no room for thought. Because if you have thoughts, you're gonna lose awareness of what's real. Practice walking in Zen, it's really nice.

~

S: Is no-mind a trick, in that we don't have to fight or strive for that? Just let thoughts be and watch?
V: Eventually that can happen. Yeah, eventually, if you just witness, you'll see enough not to want to be involved in it so you could say it is a trick. But I was very active in being present. I really, really did like

being present. At a young age, I looked around me and I could see that people who lived in their heads just suffered incredibly, the dramas that they carried on. And most of that drama is related to victim-oriented thinking. I just decided I wanted to live in reality. I gave up victim-oriented thinking completely and practised being present to what is real, because it's so peaceful to be with what's real. There's no peace being inside of your head. Not really, because you're programmed for problem solving. The idea is to get back to reality, away from the matrix of the mind, because that's the problem. There is no other problem really. It's your dreaming that's the problem. Just put awareness on what is real. Don't have to think about it. Just put awareness on what is real and stay aware of what is real.

~

S: I heard that sex causes energy and memory exchange, which causes changes in our personality and habits. So if we have sex with lower consciousness people, do we stay more in lower consciousness?

V: Not going to go anywhere near answering that question. Even if I did answer it, it would just be my opinion anyway. We are pure Beingness. We are pure awareness. Find that. Doesn't matter what the body does or doesn't do really, find that that is aware of the body, that that's aware of sex, find that and be free. Up to you. You're the one that's going to be looking. You put your awareness on sexuality, well you'll live as that. You put your awareness on Beingness, you live as that. There's a huge difference between living as Beingness and living as sex. Putting awareness on sex is a story of frustration, fulfilment, frustration, fulfilment, frustration, fulfilment. Put awareness on awareness and there's just peace, because that is our true nature.

~

S: Hi Vishrant, this is a comment only. Beingness seems so huge and palpable and present, not conceiving, not perceiving, just presence itself. Just being, I can no longer even understand how I could not have recognised it.

V: Okay. When you find Beingness as self and you decide that you want to share it with the world because you're a light, you feel like you're the man standing by the river selling water to people who are going past when all they have to do themselves is come down the river and get a drink.

~

S: How can we be aware of different things all at once?

V: Try it and see. So right now, I can be aware of this hand and I can be aware of this hand. I can be aware of my breath. I can be aware of my own voice. I can be aware of the chair I'm sitting in while aware of my hands, my breath and my voice. Why not? It's called ambient awareness. Walking in Zen is the practice of ambient awareness.

~

S: Is meditation a tool to transcend our mind or imagination and be more aware and present, and how much time does one have to meditate to achieve stillness?

V: I don't like the word transcend much. There's reality. And then there's dream. We're not trying to transcend dream. You can't transcend something that's not real in the first place, but what you can do is put your awareness on something that is real which is what meditation is. If we're doing a traditional Buddhist meditation where we're watching the breath, we're just putting awareness on the breath. We're just putting awareness on what is real. That's all we're doing. It's not about transcending anything. You can't transcend the dream, not really. Dreams aren't real. Put awareness on what's real – and everything's real except what you think. The breath is handy because if you're alive, you're breathing and it's real. So you put your awareness on it, thoughts come in, drop those, come back to the breath. Don't entertain the thoughts. Stay with the breath. This is meditation, or this is the practice of meditation. True meditation is being present to reality.

~

S: If I'm ambiently aware, I noticed my external sight being blurrier. Am I doing it right?
V: Yes. Absolutely. With ambient awareness, you're not focused. Your mind is relaxed and your eyes are relaxed, so you're not focused. In looking at a room full of people when I'm talking, people quite often think that I'm talking to them. But really, it's just ambient awareness. I'm talking to everyone, and because my mind is relaxed, my eyes are relaxed. It's just ambient awareness. And awareness is not just aware of the people and what they're doing and

saying, and all of them, it's also aware of itself. It's like having one foot in and one foot out.

~

S: Do you think that renouncing life and becoming a monk is the fastest way to become enlightened?

V: I don't know. What I do know is that someone who lives in the marketplace, who has a family, who has a job, can wake up. That I do know. Now whether it's easier to wake up in a monastery or an ashram, or easier to wake up in the marketplace, I can't actually talk about because I have never lived in a monastery. I have been in the marketplace. I have practised the meditations, I've practised the asanas, I've practised the self-inquiry, I've practised openness in the marketplace while having a family and while holding down a job. From my perspective, I'm here to teach lay people who are interested in waking up while in the marketplace so I can't really make a comment on whether it's faster or easier or better to wake up in a monastery because it's not my experience.

~

S: I contract most when I need to take action, for example, building my business or exercise. What can I do to remove these blocks and how do you properly integrate material success with spiritual success?

V: Okay, it's easier said than done. You don't be attached to either the spiritual success or the financial success. The attachment is what keeps you locked in lower consciousness, nothing else. You can be spiritually successful, if you want to call it spiritual success, which means basically your consciousness levels have risen. You can be financially successful, which basically means your bank balance is bigger or your property holdings are bigger. The attachment to them is the problem, nothing else. You can do whatever you like. It's the attachment that causes the problems. Don't be attached to be free, or be attached to be in prison. If you're frightened of losing what you've got, you're probably attached to it. Let it go. Doesn't mean that you actually have to physically let it go but, in your mind, you let it go. And you keep operating, you keep moving forward. Just because we let things go, doesn't make us redundant. We can do everything from a place of acceptance. Just try it and see.

~

S: I can see that my anger and blame is hiding helplessness, as you mentioned, that seems scary to face. What now?

V: Get brave or suffer longer and watch it more until you come to a point of witnessing where you become willing to meet it. At some point, you'll get sick of the suffering that's created by not doing something about it and you'll do something about it, but that's going to be up to you. One of my teachers used to say to people who were a bit stuck that they just haven't suffered enough. In some ways it's true. If we truly see that we're creating our own suffering and that we have a choice not to, if we truly see it, we'll probably stop it.

~

S: Is it possible to serve Truth prior to awakening?
V: Heck yeah. I started serving Truth in the 80s when I was with Rajneesh. I started serving the commune. I

started serving Osho when I was at the Ranch and in Pune. I was involved in the publishing of one of his books. But I was in service. Anybody who was interested in Truth, at that stage of my life, I'd head them towards Osho and head them towards his teachings, being in service of Truth. I wasn't setting myself up as an advisor in those days because I thought Osho really did it well. So I served Truth by turning people onto Osho from time to time. I served Truth by working for the commune. And then when the Advaita Vedanta teachers came in the late 90s, I served them. I hosted them, I hosted some of the ones that came here, and I served them. I served them in helping them in publishing as well. And continuing to serve people by turning them towards satsang. So yes, you can definitely serve Truth before Enlightenment. Anybody who's teaching the dharma is serving Truth. Anybody who's helping someone who's teaching the dharma is serving Truth.

~

S: What would you say is the most significant lifestyle change you made that then led to Enlightenment?
V: The most significant lifestyle change I made is I walked in one day and gave all my companies to my staff because I could see clearly that for me, as a businessman, the way my mind was programmed, it wasn't gonna work – and higher consciousness was calling. I could see that my warlike nature as a businessman was in the way of my Heart, and in the way of awakening, so I consciously chose to give it all away and pursue Heart. That was a major change in life

because it meant giving away a multimillion-dollar company and becoming a bum and walking around Australia as a bum for four years in search of my Heart, and I have never had one regret at doing that.

S: Does that mean you saw that you're attached to your businesses, you are saying we can do anything, but not have attachments?

V: Even though I'd retired years before, I was still running them remotely, from actually England at the time. And I knew I could feel this connection, this chord that I had with them, and it was keeping me in a state of mind that was semi-warlike, because business at a high level is war and I didn't want it. I had been programmed to be like that in my schooling. I'd done a myriad of courses to get better and bigger, better and more powerful. And it was all in action, and I just needed not to be in action. I needed to do nothing. I needed to have that not in my life anymore. I'm not saying that other people can't keep their businesses. That's fine. It just for me, the way I had been programmed, I needed to get rid of it. I needed it to go. I could see clearly it was an obstacle in my way.

~

S: Once you know about what it takes to go for Enlightenment, can you really be happy just living a mundane life?

V: The point of no return, when you know too much. It is best if you start this journey that you finish it. Because you can get quite bitter and discontent if you put a lot of effort into it and you don't finish it. Anybody that starts should finish. It's best. There's nothing better than raising your consciousness levels and there's nothing better than finding Heart. Not really. It's so beautiful to love, and in raising our consciousness levels, we remove all of the obstacles that are in the way of Heart. So we start to serve Heart too which is very beautiful, but that's up to you. What do you serve? Who do you serve? I found that self-service was dissatisfying and then in service of Heart I found what I referred to as manageable happiness – the beauty of being in service, the beauty of taking care of others, the beauty of taking care of plants, animals, the planet. It's just lovely. Whereas self-obsession, taking care of self, is not lovely. In selfless service, we start setting ourselves up for Enlightenment, because we're removing the problem. We're removing the "I". It's up to you. What do you serve? Who do you serve? Does it bring you happiness? If it doesn't, well you're probably on the wrong path.

~

S: Thank you for your simple answers. I would like to know about meditation. What is the best technique for beginners?

V: You know, it's hard just to sit down and watch the breath unless you've done a fair bit of it. The best method of meditation is walking because if we're walking, and we're aware of everything outside of ourselves, but not our thoughts, we're in meditation. If we can put our awareness on our breath while we're walking, if we can put our awareness on our footfalls when we're walking, as we walk and our visuals, more than likely that will be enough to keep us in meditation. The only time we move out of meditation is when we start thinking again and we have our awareness on thoughts. But if we can put our awareness on enough things that are real while in action, we're in meditation.

We're starting to get an idea of what it's like to be in meditation again because up until about four or five, we were in meditation. As little kids, we were present to reality. We weren't dreaming yet. We weren't problem solving yet. We weren't projecting as much yet. It's like going back to a childlike state where we're in wonderment with the world because we're not thinking about it, we're with it. In the beginning, the walking meditation is very effective, and from that, you can go to the sitting meditation. With a sitting meditation, I found that Rajneesh's active meditations – dynamic meditation and kundalini meditation – were really excellent because they helped clear the energy of the day before I was able to sit. When we clear all of the energy of the day we can sit and then really relax and be with what's real, in this case, the breath.

And so you can begin with walking meditation. That's a nice meditation and nobody needs to know you're meditating. You're just walking. You don't do it listening to music. You just listen to nature and you just see nature and you feel nature. And you feel your breath and you feel your footfalls. And now you're with reality, you've moved away from the matrix of the mind. You're in meditation. It's an active meditation. If you want to do other meditations, the Rajneesh meditations of dynamic and kundalini are really effective. I did them for years. They're really effective. It's up to you. They keep you fit as well. It's up to you. Meditation is the way out of the matrix of the mind. It's the best thing you can do for you.

Thank you for satsang. Good to see you bravehearts here today.

CHAPTER SIX

The Light of Awareness

V: Welcome to satsang.
S: Hello Vishrant, can you please talk about the light of awareness?
V: So, when there is no awareness, we're in the dark, we're in lower consciousness. We just run automatically and unconsciously according to whatever default patterns we may have. When we become more aware, when there is more awareness of what's happening, there is the potential for not running true to default patterning. There's the potential for seeing things that may be causing detriment in our lives and not running them. When we look at consciousness levels in human beings, from lower consciousness to higher consciousness to superconsciousness, we're looking at quite a range. When it comes to animals, they're pretty much running to default patterns that they have no control over. They just have to do them, but as human beings, we have the ability to raise our consciousness levels, to see through the mind and to react or not react. In other words, respond. This is the beauty of higher consciousness: we can see what our mind is up to because we know what it's doing. We can actually not get involved in activities of the mind that hurt us or hurt other human beings. So the light of awareness is really just seeing – clearly

seeing what is going on because we're aware of it. We're not lost in some dream. We're seeing reality. We're seeing what's really going on.

For me, I sought out awakened teachers. I sought out awakened people. The first one, my spiritual master and my spiritual father, was Osho Rajneesh who called himself Bhagwan Shree Rajneesh when I first joined him in 1982. And he had this light of awareness about him. He illuminated everything for me, made me question everything, made me check out all of my belief systems that I had taken for granted for so long that turned out not to be true. The light of awareness shone and I got to see things that I didn't like about myself. I got to see things that I did like about myself, but now I could see what was going on in my own mind, clearly, I started to have a choice as to whether I would run those programs or not. And this I afford to the light of awareness illuminated by Osho Rajneesh.

Most people, including myself, have not been programmed to be happy. We were probably programmed to be efficient little machines, going to school and learning how to problem solve. But I can't remember anywhere in my schooling where I was taught or programmed on how to be happy. It's so funny because that's what everyone on the planet wants. Everybody here on earth wants to be happy, yet it's not taught at school, so we pursue things in an endeavour to make ourselves happy. Usually, we pursue wealth or success in something, we pursue relationships, we pursue the ownership of objects –

houses, cars, whatever else – thinking that in some way these things will make us happy. But they in themselves are desires which make us unhappy because any desire is resistance to what is, which is a form of suffering. We don't realise that we can't find happiness outside of ourselves yet. We keep looking outside of ourselves for it, thinking if we get more of this or less of this or a better relationship or we are more loving in relationship or something, you know, something outside, that we'll find happiness.

True happiness is inside of ourselves when we find Heart, when we find Beingness as self, the two ways I know. One is to find the love that is here, which is covered by our closure and defendedness. The other is to find our true nature, pure awareness as self, because then the mind experiences profound contentment for no reason which is my definition of happiness. The light of awareness shining on the mind, the mind just rests – just rests, profoundly content for no reason. But none of us were programmed for this at school. None of us were taught how to be happy. None of us were taught how to become enlightened. I don't think any of us were really even taught how to find our own Hearts or what's in the way of us experiencing our own Hearts. So as adults, we have to start questioning. What's it all about? What's going on? What's really worth something here? And what is not? These questions are the questions of the seeker. Who am I really?

Any questions, any statements, any challenges to this teaching today?

S: The first question is as follows: you were speaking of the pursuit of happiness outside of ourselves, gathering material things, relationships, experiences – what can make people pursue happiness in a way that really works?

V: The recognition that we can't find happiness outside of ourselves takes away a great deal of the problem. Our constant desiring of things to be different than how they are is actually a form of suffering. Yet we're programmed to believe that if we're ambitious for things, for life, for success, this is a good thing. Wow, have we really examined what ambition is? Have we really examined how much discontentment there is in being ambitious? And if it becomes a default pattern – and in most people who are ambitious, it does, it never stops – it just runs continuously until the person dies. I feel sorry for people who are ambitious because I know that they are suffering more than most. Yet in the West, we admire them. "Oh, an ambitious man, an ambitious woman, they're getting somewhere." Well, they're not getting happiness. Ambition equals suffering, not happiness. To know you have enough brings a certain level of happiness. To constantly want more is misery.

~

S: How can I measure how conscious I am?

V: Okay. So if someone disagrees with you or does something that you don't like or there's something happening in the world that you don't like and you contract towards that, go into resistance towards that, it means there's some unconsciousness there, because if you're truly conscious, you don't contract, you don't resist, you accept life as it is. That does not make you ineffective. It just means you accept life as it is, while still being effective in the material world. If you're contracting over life, there's a place where you're unconscious, there's a place where you haven't shown up with acceptance and love. Just the practice of openness as a teaching towards higher consciousness in itself is so brilliant. Every time you find yourself closing or contracting or resisting life, open up and undo any belief system that supports that contraction, that resistance. Open up, and if you open up enough, you'll find Heart, the true jewel of consciousness which is always here. It's just veiled by a mind full of thoughts, full of defence systems, full of closures, full of resistances. Openness truly counts for everything. Practice openness. It's brilliant. It does mean though that you're going to be undefended. It does mean that you're going to be vulnerable because you're going to be open. But this is the Way of the Heart. Being defended, being closed, being resistant, is the way of the mind. A very different path. Sometimes they talk about the least-travelled path. From my perspective, the least-travelled path for most human beings is the Way of the Heart: to live in the world open, vulnerable, with your Heart on your sleeve. You do get to receive love and you will get hurt from time to time, but what a beautiful way to live. Because when Heart is perceived, the way it affects the mind is you want to take care of everything and everybody. This is the noble path.

~

S: What did it take for you to be completely happy with what you've got all of the time?

V: You probably won't like the answer for this one. The answer is very simple: an absence of "I". See the "I" has a lot of trouble being happy. It's its nature to be unhappy in some ways because it's constantly wanting things to be different, which is unhappiness, it's discontentment, so the less "I", the more happiness. A wonderful Buddhist saying, "Less 'I' less problems," and it's true. No "I", no problem.

When you start opening up and you start perceiving the beauty of love and Heart, you start to fall into service. It's just natural to fall into service because you just want to help people. Now, the more you fall into service, the less "I" there is because you put yourself aside for the benefit of whatever else you're doing. Maybe helping a person, or an animal. It could be a plant. It could just be vacuuming the floor, but you've put yourself in the service. You as an "I" have taken a backseat. The less "I", the happier you can be because the "I" is not a happy thing. It's not there all of the time. People think, "Oh my ego is here all of the time". No it's not. It's only there when there's ownership. You can go through a lot of the day without an "I" and operate perfectly well in the world, but people who are self-obsessed, people who are selfish have a strong "I" present a lot of the time and as a result, they suffer a lot of the time. I think the Way of the Heart is the only way to live on this planet. So open up, open up, open up and support Heart. Then that affects your mind and you find you just want to take care of everything and everyone. A beautiful way to live. But that's up to you. Nobody can make you do anything you don't want to do. It's up to you. You're the one who has to open up. You're the one who has to be vulnerable. You're the one who has to be undefended. It's up to you.

S: Why do you talk about opening your Heart, instead of opening your third eye?

~

V: I talk about both, it's just that if we were in a monastery or an ashram, where we weren't in the marketplace, where we didn't have to deal with people, we could just concentrate on discipline, concentrate on the jnani path, meditation, putting awareness on the third eye or the crown, self-inquiry, asanas, all of the different things that can be done towards Enlightenment. But because we're in the marketplace and we're not monks and we're not nuns and we're not sadhus, because we're in the marketplace, we have to live a certain way, and the Way of the Heart is way more beautiful than any other way to live in the marketplace.

I see those who are interested in Enlightenment need two wings to fly. One is the wing of discipline, meditation, self-inquiry, the practice of openness, the practice of undoing beliefs, a certain discipline. The other way is the wing of love. And we achieve love or we perceive love by putting ourselves aside, by being less than, by being open, by being undefended. And with these two wings, we can operate in the marketplace towards Enlightenment. So I teach both.

~

S: Are your consciousness levels still rising?
V: I have no interest in consciousness levels. The experience or the knowing or what's here is just this. It needs absolutely nothing. It is perfect in every way. It was never born, it cannot die, and it cannot be touched by anything. Consciousness levels are related to the mind and there is just no interest in it.

~

S: I enjoy being in service sometimes, but not others. What stops me from going into service all of the time?
V: It's a choice. I remember when I decided that it would be a good idea to serve Heart after experiencing some awakenings of the Heart where I felt that unconditional love for everybody and everything. I wasn't experiencing that because I was too closed. I realised that, well, if I'm going to serve Heart, I've got to find a way to find Heart again, I've got to undo me as an "I", undo me as a psyche so I can experience the beauty of love and then allow love to dictate how I live my life. And when love started dictating the way I lived, I just wanted to help everybody. Up until then, though, I recognised that that's how love would affect my mind, even though sometimes it wasn't because it wasn't being perceived. And so I would actually do it anyway, I would serve Heart. I had a practice of taking care of others, whether it was my family, my friends, my client base, strangers in the street, it didn't matter. I just wanted to find a way to lift everybody I met. This is the Way of the Heart.

~

S: Why are awakened people often said to be carrying the light?

V: Okay, so someone who's awake has awareness aware of itself or consciousness conscious of itself or Beingness aware of itself, which has absolutely nothing to do with the mind. There is something in all human beings that is aware and usually it's aware of the mind and what the mind is thinking and through the senses the world. And it's not aware of itself, but it's there. In someone who's awake, this that's aware of the mind is also aware of itself and when it becomes aware of itself or conscious of itself, there is a field of energy produced called a Buddha field. And for those who are sensitive, it is palpable, it can be very easily perceived. From my perspective, with the people that I was interested in, they carried this energy field, because I had fallen in love with this energy field around Osho. The energy field itself, the Buddha field created by awareness aware of itself, is really our own true nature, and so I would tune into that field of energy. It would open my third eye, it would open my crown chakra, it would open my Heart chakra because I surrendered to that field of energy. It in itself is a doorway to your own nature, to your own true nature. Sometimes it's called the light of awareness. Sometimes it's said that people who are awake carry this light, but that is the light. It is the Buddha field that is created by awareness being aware of itself in a human being. If that Buddha field is not there, that person is not awake no matter what they sound like or what they do. The only way you can really detect if someone is awake is if they have a continuous 24-hour-a-day Buddha field.

~

S: Is everything you tell us coming from the Heart or from the thinking mind?

V: Pretty much every single thing I talk about comes from direct experience. I don't talk about anything that is not directly experienced here. One of the failings I found in my seeking in the early days was I tended to believe people who were further ahead than me, rather than looking for myself, and that was a big mistake. You have to look for yourself. You have to look inside yourself for the answers and if they are your experience, then it is your knowing. And so I speak from my own knowing of what is real and what is not real. My intention is to help people get free.

As far as Heart's concerned, Heart doesn't direct anything, Heart just loves. It doesn't have another capacity. Quite often people project onto Heart that it does all sorts of things, that it even thinks and talks, but it doesn't. Heart just loves, and when that love affects the mind, then the mind will try to take care of everybody and everything because that's how love affects the mind. But I talk from inner knowing, and love is here, but I can't say that I'm talking from love because I can't even find an "I" that could own that love. This is one of the things people don't understand about Enlightenment. You as an "I" don't ever, ever, ever wake up. You can't, because you're a

dream. That that's aware of the "I" becomes aware of itself. That is awakening and the "I" surrenders. It lays down. It's over. The masquerade has finished.
S: How come we trust the thoughts, if we learn how not to trust our mind?
V: Ha, I got to a stage before awakening where I trusted silence and stillness and nothing else. And the reason I got to that stage was I recognised that the mind or the ego part of the mind was trying to survive because Enlightenment is the annihilation of the "I". So it would try to survive by creating problems by little helper thoughts, so from my perspective, what occurred was a non-trusting of the mind anymore. As a matter of fact, there was no touching of the mind anymore. Awareness was continually turned back to itself until it locked on to itself. The mind with the mind and its story, even its helpers, had become absolutely irrelevant and were surrendered.

~

S: Is higher consciousness necessary for waking up?
V: Heck yeah! Well, you have a look at lower consciousness. Lower consciousness means you're caught in a dream, which is based on programming you receive from mum and dad, your peers, your schooling, your government, your religion – and none of those things involve freedom. They usually involve you resisting life and being a victim to life in some way. Locked in lower consciousness does not support superconsciousness. Higher consciousness supports superconsciousness. And so, the work – if you want to see it as work – for the seeker is actually

to produce a mind that will support superconsciousness, Enlightenment. A mind that is locked in lower consciousness is only going to support suffering. Look for yourself and see.

~

S: When closer to awakening, doesn't the "I" still benefit in that the "I" feels happier or more blissful?
V: That's an idea, not a reality. The "I" disappears. There's just space. There's just looking, but nobody looking. If there's walking, there's walking, but nobody walking. If there's talking, there's talking, but there's nobody talking. There's an absence, and that absence is lovely. It's not the "I" that gets anything from Enlightenment. It's not a party it can come to. It surrenders unconditionally. It gives up its story. That's freedom.

~

S: When you say that you surrendered to the Buddha field of your teacher, how did you surrender to it?
V: I tuned into the field of energy because I could perceive it and I allowed it to annihilate me. I allowed it to open every part up inside of me. I allowed it like the wind blowing through me. I gave my life to it eventually. Because really, what we are is just everything or nothing, but it's everything and nothing. And the definition of everything or omnipotence is God. And when we give ourselves totally to that, we start to find we are that, but not as a personal "I", just as pure awareness, pure consciousness, pure Beingness. Whatever the mind puts first, it tends to live as. When the mind puts Beingness first, or pure

awareness first, or God first, that's what we tend to live as. Up to you. Where do you put your awareness?

~

S: What does the phrase, "Become a light so others can see" mean?

V: "Become a light so others can see" simply means you wake up so others can find themselves as Truth, so others can see. It is a complete sacrifice because if you wake up, you sacrifice the "I" to wake up. And so Enlightenment is not a selfish thing. It can't be. It can't be for self because, first of all, self is not real, the "I" is not real. You wake up so others can see. You surrender yourself so others can see. You give yourself to God so others can see. You give yourself to Truth so others can see. Because when awakening occurs in you, there's a Buddha field produced and in this Buddha field, people can find their minds slowing down. They can find their minds relaxing. They can start to find the background as themselves. And so you become a walking light so others can see, when awakening occurs. This is a very beautiful way to live. But it's not for you. It's for others. There's no such thing as selfish Enlightenment. That's not a possibility.

~

S: Is it better for this path to be with people's pain, to accept and open my Heart, or be with higher consciousness people to feel a higher vibration?

V: Why not both? Why give me an alternative there? Why not be with both? Why not be with everybody? Why be so fussy? As you open up, you will take the pain of other people. That's just what happens. If

you really want to raise your consciousness quickly, hang out with people who are further ahead than you. It's simple. It's a bit like any kind of sport. If you want to get good at any kind of sport, play against people who are better than you. The same goes with higher consciousness. If you really want to raise your consciousness levels, hang out with people who are further ahead than you. It's the way this is, the whole idea of the master-disciple relationship. The disciple comes to the master who's further ahead, hangs out with them, and there's a transmission – and in the transmission, there's awakening for the disciple. The disciple has chosen to be with someone who's further ahead so they can wake up. This works. It's up to you. The people who you hang out with will affect you. There's no doubt about that. It's always best, no matter what you're doing, to be with people who are going in the same direction as you, always. But that's up to you. From my perspective, I liked to hang out with awakened people because that's the fast way. That's the freeway. It can be very uncomfortable though because you're going to get shown all of the things that are in the way. All of the obstacles are going to get shown, and more than likely you're attached to them. So, it's really a matter of learning to accept life and learning to let go of everything.
~

S: Can just sitting in the presence of an awakened person change your consciousness levels?
V: Did for me. When I sat with Rajneesh, I sat and interviewed him for 48 minutes in 1985 and I never

recovered from that interview. I was never the same again. I lost the ambition for business and grew such a strong thirst for Truth, such a strong thirst to get free. I was never the same. I think that if you're fortunate enough to come into the presence of someone who's awake, you are very fortunate.

~

S: Can being in service to an enlightened person take you to higher consciousness and Enlightenment?
V: I believe that's true. And the reason I believe that to be true is I have a firm understanding that karma is real. Whatever we put into life, we get back. And so, we have negative and positive karma, depending on how we're living our lives. To be involved in trying to help other people get free would have to be good karma. The Buddha, Gautama the Buddha, stated that the highest karma a human being can attain is to teach the dharma. In other words, to teach the teachings that help people get free. I tend to agree. When you support somebody who is actually teaching the dharma, helping people to get free, you are gaining good karma for yourself. But of course, the same goes for if you try running someone down who's trying to get people free. If you try discrediting them in some way, if you turn people away from them, I think that would attract a certain sort of karma as well. And that wouldn't be so positive.

~

S: Is it in everyone's interest to become awake?
V: I'm a total fatalist. If you're awake, you're meant to be awake. If you're not awake, you're not meant to

be awake. People like this idea of a quickening where everything is moving towards awakening in a faster way. I don't see it that way. I see life as it is and I accept life as it is. This is what is: I'm not interested in projecting what should or shouldn't be onto life. Life is just the way it is. Whatever happens is meant to happen, otherwise, it would not have happened.

~

S: Is it part of the process when we hear sounds, for example, the sound of the earth or space, when we meditate or when we quieten down?

V: Okay. I understand the question. But my interest in meditation was more about putting awareness on what was real rather than what was not real. So whether it was a sound, or whether it was the breath coming in and out at my lip, or whether it was my footfalls, my interest was in being present to reality. It didn't matter what that reality was, as long as it was reality. The only thing that is not real is what you think. Meditation, true meditation, really occurs in no-mind when our awareness is just present to what is real. So whether you put your awareness on the sounds or on anything else, it doesn't matter, as long as it's real – and then be present to reality all of the time.

~

S: If karma is in charge, so to speak, then are all of our efforts in vain?

V: Look, if you go to any Buddhist monastery in the world and you speak to the ajhans as a layperson, and you say, "Ajahn, what can I do to become enlightened?" from my experience, what they'll tell you is you need to become more generous, more kind. And the reason they say that is because they believe that you need good karma to even hear the Truth, to even become a monk. And you gain good karma by being a nice person. It counters all the negative karma you might have picked up when you weren't so nice. And so, I teach people the Way the Heart, and really, if you look at the Way of the Heart, it's just lovely to take care of other human beings. It's lovely to be in service to the plants, to the animals, to the planet, to vacuuming the floor, because when we're giving – and this is giving – we are accruing good karma.

Unfortunately, we live in a world where there's a lot of selfishness. There's a lot of self-obsession. And you see that in all of the wars, you see it in all of the rapes, all of the murders, all of the lies, all of the cheating. You see, if people were in touch with their Hearts, we wouldn't even need a police force, let alone an army. But there's a lack of Heart on this planet. There is only one sin. I know the Christian religions have lots of sins. So do the Muslim religions, but there's only one sin. It's selfishness. If you are selfless, you are sinless. And you take care of everybody and everything. This is beautiful. This way of living raises your consciousness levels. This way of living gives you good karma.

You talked about karma being in control, of being controlled by karma. You're the one who produces it. You're the one who's doing it. Sometimes they talk about people waking up at a very young age, you know, at birth or very young. My understanding is that, very clearly, this person has brought that karma in from previous lives. This isn't the first time they played this game. It's all karma. It's all energy balancing out. Just being able to hear someone talk about Truth says that you have good karma, otherwise you wouldn't be able to hear it.

~

S: Is it good to look back at the past and think that it was all fate?
V: There is a great saying "those who do not remember the past are doomed to repeat it". And so, we can learn a great deal of lessons on how to be in this world from remembering our past. But in the same breath, remembering is dream. It's beautiful just to be here without any dream. It's beautiful to be that fresh, to be that in the moment, without any dream. When you are little kids, up to the age of about three, that's where you live, just here. Very few projections, very few memories, just here. And as adults, we can come back to this space of reality, which is meditation, if we're willing to abandon the dream. And if we look at what meditation is, or formal meditation, it's abandoning the dream for what is real, until what is real becomes our default pattern. Being aware of what is real. Then meditation is every moment being here, being here, being here. Your choice.

~

S: Is tuning into the energy of the Buddha field and witnessing the mind enough to awaken?
V: You could say yes. If you're tuning into the Buddha field and expanding your own consciousness

and using the clarity of the energy field to watch the mind, you can see all of the things that are working or not working. This gives you the opportunity to run them or not run them. Yes. So, witnessing the mind is a way to Enlightenment because in the witnessing, in becoming more conscious of the mind – which is higher consciousness – you don't get caught in the mind. Instead of reacting, you're now responding, so it is a way to Enlightenment. Osho Rajneesh taught witnessing of the mind and I would agree.

I like self-inquiry for people as well. Turning awareness back to itself, asking the question „Who is aware?" or "What's aware?" That works as well. But if you don't witness the mind, you're going to keep getting caught in it. You're going to get caught in its stories and its dramas. As a witness to the mind, there's detachment from the mind so you don't get caught, and as a result of not being caught, you can respond instead of react. And so, I think witnessing is wonderful as a methodology towards higher consciousness and Enlightenment. I like the combination of witnessing the mind and self-inquiry, along with openness to support the Heart. I think it's a neat mixture that works.

~

S: If we begin to serve Heart, do we become a light for others?
V: Yes you do, because if you begin to serve Heart, you will take care of others. It's just how Heart affects the mind. It's just how love affects the mind. You will become a light, yes.

~

S: Can the light of awareness bring up and heal the dark night of the soul?

V: The problem with the light of awareness for people is if you come into the presence of someone who's awake, it does expand your mind. You do find more silence, you find stillness, you find the third eye starting to open, you find the crown starting to open, but you also find that all of the coping mechanisms that have held down all of your pain bodies for your lifetimes start to become undone as well. And so in the presence of someone who's awake, you start to open up, and everything that's inside that has been kept prisoner for lifetimes starts to emerge. Carl Jung called this the dark night of the soul. And it can very much be the dark night of the soul. What's required during that process is acceptance. You allow it to occur, you be tenderly okay with whatever appears, and it will come and it will go. The problem is we are programmed for comfort. We're programmed to avoid pain and chase pleasure, and because of this, we tend to avoid our own wounding which stops us from healing our own wounding. But as you go up and up and up in consciousness levels, you need to heal your wounding. You need to be okay with it. You need to be okay with everything. So when the dark night of the soul occurs, you be okay with it and everything comes out. It's like an old friend you've had in prison for years leaves. But that's up to you. It does mean that you'd have to be willing to experience discomfort because it's not comfortable to feel your pain bodies. And that's up to you: you either are or you aren't.

~

S: The following question is from a viewer: how does one heal the wounding?

V: Ah, I just described that. Yes, we heal the wounding simply by allowing ourselves to feel it. We can't heal wounding in any other way that I know. And the reason that people are wounded is because they have wounding inside of them that they're not willing to feel because if we were willing to feel it, we'd heal it. We create wounding ourselves quite often by victim-orientated thinking: turning ourselves into victims of something and then compounding it by entertaining our story over and over again in different ways. But if we're prepared to feel what's there, if we're prepared to be tenderly okay with whatever appears, we can heal it. But the operative word is tender. Not just okay. Tenderly, okay. And if we can feel it, we can heal it. Up to you though. Because inside of wounding is not just pain, there's quite often hopelessness and helplessness, and these are feelings we really don't want to know about because they touch on our survival. But they're the feelings we also have to be prepared to feel. And so, it's up to you. How much courage do you have to actually feel, to be tenderly okay with whatever is inside of you?

~

S: When we attempt to turn awareness onto Beingness, is it perceivable that we are heading in the right direction?

V: If you start turning your awareness onto itself, and you start discovering that you are that awareness, wow, is your life going to be different. That's actually what happened to me in 1987, two years after interviewing Osho. Awareness became aware of itself while walking on the beach, beach front or river front in Applecross, Perth, Western Australia, asking the question, "Who am I?" And I found myself as the universe. Well, you get a taste of that and nothing's the same ever again because it's really, really clear that you are not an "I". You never were and you cannot be and what you actually really are is just awesome.

~

S: When you began to let go of your attachments and therefore not grab on to every thought and impulse that came along, was there a period of boredom? Is that normal?

V: First of all, I didn't really let go of my attachments. They let go of me because I put Truth first. And in putting Truth first, everything else dropped away. With regards to boredom, because we are so used to entertaining our mind with constant rubbish talk, when it stops, the mind can get bored. And one of my teachers asked me, after awakening, "Are you prepared to be bored for the rest of your life?" I recognised what he was saying because the mind was addicted to entertainment and I just made that absolutely okay. Absolutely okay forever and ever. The key to higher consciousness, the key to Enlightenment, is unconditional surrender, nothing else.

~

S: So does healing the wounding through tender acceptance mean separating the emotion that arises from the thought or feeling that created the painful emotion? That is, not going with a story from the past?

V: You've got to be careful of the story, because the story is probably victim-orientated, which means it'll be used to create more wounding. And so, part of healing the wounding is allowing yourself to feel what's there, to be tenderly okay with what's there without wounding yourself again with some story about how hard done by you were. In healing wounding, we have to remove the thing that keeps topping the wounding up and that'll be the belief system in victim-orientated thinking, and that's reasonably difficult to do. But it's absolutely possible. We are not victims. Victims volunteer to be victims. Things happen. And we can volunteer to be a victim, or we can just see this is what happens. This is what is. The moment we become a victim of it, we've started to wound ourselves. Remove all victim orientation. See life as "this is just what it is" neither good nor bad. It's just what it is. This cannot wound you and it also ends the story of drama.

So, the two things involved in healing the wounds of the Heart are the willingness to be tenderly okay with whatever is appearing and also the willingness to not be a victim.

~

S: I just watched the video about desires in the channel and I want to know which ones of our wishes we could still consider good and try to feed and support or we just never want?

V: Yeah, I hear the question and I would like to promote one desire. I would like to promote the desire you have to wake up, the desire that you have to be free, because that one desire is the only worthy desire that we can have. If we don't recognise we're in prison, we don't even want to get out. But once we recognise we're imprisoned, the desire to get out is the only thing that is going to support us getting out. And so that thirst for Truth has to be fired up to a level where you will move to action to make it so. There is no other way. All other desires? Don't put too much emphasis on them, otherwise they'll create suffering in you. The more strongly you addictively demand anything, the more suffering there is, and that even goes for the desire to be free. But it is the only desire that is worth having. There is no other desire that's really as valuable as that one because that's the one that can get you out of prison. That's the one that will motivate you to do whatever you need to do to get free. And so awake teachers are really there to point people in the right direction and to fire up the thirst for freedom. This is the true revolution.

Thank you for satsang. Good to see you bravehearts here today.

CHAPTER SEVEN

What is Required to Wake Up

V: Welcome to satsang.
S: What is required to wake up?
V: The very thing that wants to wake up, the ego, actually can't wake up because awakening is when that that is aware of the mind becomes aware of itself, which actually has nothing to do with the ego, the "I". So the "I" can never really wake up, but what it can do is facilitate an environment where awakening can occur. The work for the seeker is to remove any obstacle that is in the way of awakening, using methodologies like self-inquiry and meditation to turn awareness back to itself so awareness can lock on to itself and stay on itself.

Someone who's enlightened has that which is aware of the mind aware of itself continuously 24 hours a day, seven days a week. For most human beings, awareness that's aware of the mind is just that: aware of the mind and through the senses, the body and the world. Someone who's awake has managed to turn awareness back to itself. The "I" doesn't really get to come to that party, because the "I" itself without imagination doesn't exist. It's a dream. But it can assist by self-inquiring, asking the question "Who's aware?" or "What's aware?" It can also assist by removing any obstacles creating resistance or contraction in the mind which attracts awareness to itself. This would mean removing belief systems that have expectations attached to them. When those expectations aren't met, contraction and resistance to life can occur. In removing or undoing the belief systems, there can be freedom from that form of resistance.

So, we go on and on and on. How do we wake up? The "I" thinks, well, I'll wake up. No, the "I" doesn't wake up. Awakening can occur at any time. A satori can occur at any time. You could be doing Sufi whirling, you could be meditating, you could be walking on a beach, you could be getting up from the breakfast table. It doesn't matter because reality is always here. Pure awareness is always here and when it gets a glimpse of itself, it gives you an understanding that, heck, we're not just an "I", there's something else here. Those who meditate, who find no-mind, find that they're there, but there's nobody there. There's no "I" there. There's just pure awareness. So, what is this that is purely aware? That is what is interesting to the seeker. And the question of course, is "Who am I?" Really, who am I?

So the seeker investigates and usually gets involved in studying books, YouTube videos, trying to collect knowledge, so they can understand their way to Enlightenment. Of course, that does not work. You cannot understand your way to Enlightenment because understanding is the booby prize. It just creates a knowledgeable ego. What is aware of that knowledgeable ego? What is aware of it, that's of interest. Who are you really? And so it is only in practice that people wake up: the practice of self-inquiry, the practice of meditation, the practice of openness and the practice of removing all obstacles that are in the way that create contraction in the mind and attracts awareness back to itself.

You look at these contractions. The mind contracts, awareness goes to it. So if the mind even finds awareness when it's turning awareness back to itself, it starts to witness it, it starts to try to own it, and in that very ownership, it loses it. The mind has to let go. What's required is unconditional surrender. The mind needs to give itself to Truth. The mind of the "I" says "Thy will be done, not my will" and it surrenders. It surrenders to Truth. It gives itself to Truth. And that works, if the mind is actually ready, if the mind has been prepared to support Enlightenment. A mind that is constantly contracting and resisting life has not been prepared properly yet. The likelihood is that even if awareness is aware of itself, even if consciousness is aware of itself, awareness is going to be coming back to the mind when the mind starts contracting and resisting.

So you look and see. What works and what doesn't work? It took me a long time to realise that the collecting of knowledge doesn't work. You can't raise your consciousness levels and you can't become enlightened by collecting knowledge. Even if the knowledge is good, it's not going to help that much. The only bit of knowledge that you need to know is that unconditional surrender is the doorway to

Enlightenment. Self-inquiry will facilitate it, meditation will facilitate it, the practice of openness will facilitate it. All of these things are up to you. You really want to wake up? You need to do what you need to do to make it so.

Are there any questions, any statements, any challenges to this teaching today?

S: How can I deepen my love affair with Truth so that my mind will surrender to it?

V: Okay, so I can only talk about the experience that happened here, and that was that I got curious. I wanted to know what it was all about. What is this Enlightenment thing? What is this higher consciousness thing? I'd been curious about personal growth before that and it turns out that a lot of the things that involve personal growth also support higher consciousness, like removing belief systems that are limiting, undoing anything that creates resistance in you. Any kind of failure pattern needs to be looked at and undone. So it's up to you, it's up to you, completely up to you. You actually have to look and see. For me, I started to watch the mind, and in witnessing the mind, I started to see, hmm, there's something here that's aware of the mind. There's something else here. What's this that's aware? And then I got caught back into analysing the mind and collecting knowledge and listening to teachers because I was only curious at that stage, the love affair hadn't developed yet. Then in satsang with Osho Rajneesh, I started to experience some of the silence and stillness that was around him. And there was a beauty because it was peaceful. I would come to satsang in the morning and I'd go to darshan at night, and I just fell in love with the silence and the stillness and the peace. It was just beautiful.

Then after a few years, I started having what's called satoris. I had a major satori, where, while walking on the beach one day asking the question "Who am I?" I discovered self as the universe, just every particle of everything that existed. And my mind went, wow, I want more of that. I want to know that. That became my beloved, from the mind's perspective. And I just wanted to be one with the beloved. And so, in examining the mind, I started to see what was creating the separation, and it was the dream of "I". And so self-inquiry continued. "Who's aware? What's aware? Who am I?" The "I" was dismissed in meditation. It was dismissed in self-inquiry. The space was beginning to be found. The love affair from the mind to Beingness, the beloved, was becoming stronger and stronger. Then some teachers came eight years after Osho died, and the moment they walked in the room, awakening occurred again, Enlightenment, satori, self as everything. It's hard to describe: self as everything and nothing. The mind was so infatuated, it was prepared to give itself to Truth. It so wanted to be one with Truth, the beloved, it gave itself to Truth.

~

S: Without satori, do you think it's possible to fall in love with the beloved?

V: I don't know. It's not my experience, though I can say this: before satori, before I started having satoris –

because it was about four years after I met Osho that I started having satoris – before I had satoris, I actually had fallen in love with Osho because he was beautiful and because the presence was beautiful. And so I was in love with the image of the teacher, and you've got to remember, the teacher was carrying the presence, was carrying Beingness, was exhibiting externally in presence what we are, and I had fallen in love with that.

~

S: Do you encourage your students to focus on their love affair with you?

V: Not really. If someone falls in love, they fall in love. If they don't, they don't. When you find someone who's carrying the presence, if you're fortunate enough to fall in love with them, you've fallen in love with a doorway that can show you Truth, can show you your true nature. I had met awakened people before I met Osho and I wasn't impressed. There wasn't something there for me. It just didn't click. When I met Osho, it clicked, it felt right. I was very impressed by him. And after a while, I fell in love with him. He's a very beautiful person. And so, if people fall in love with what's here, so be it. If they don't, so be it. I don't encourage anybody. It's up to the individual. What do they find when they move into the presence here? What's here for them? I'm such a fatalist. If it's meant to be, it will be. If it is not meant to be, it will not be.

~

S: What is the best approach to removing limiting beliefs? Thank you.

V: If we develop a witness to our mind that just watches the mind, we get to see all of the different beliefs that come into play, that make up who we think we are, where we think we're going, how we should behave, how other people should behave. And we can see that some of these beliefs create contraction in us when their expectations aren't met. From my perspective, any belief that creates a contraction because an expectation is not met is a limiting belief because it's keeping us locked in lower consciousness. The moment we put doubt into a belief system, we start undoing the belief system. In examining beliefs, we can ask the question about the belief. Is it true? Is it true in the big picture of everything? And if there's any doubt there, we have found the doorway to undo that belief. All beliefs have doubt unless we firmly have faith in them, and that faith is going to keep us locked in lower consciousness. Challenge all belief systems. The best answer we can ever come up with is "I don't know" because that's a more honest answer. But it doesn't make us feel safe to say "I don't know". It makes us safe to say, "Yeah, I know, I know, I know". But then we're closed the moment we say "I know". We're closed. We've cut ourselves off. If we say "I don't know", we've allowed ourselves to remain open. We've become like little children again, open and fresh so the universe can pour through us. We're not caught thinking we know. We're not stuck, and this is probably one of the biggest downfalls of the seeker, thinking or believing that we know. Studying a whole pile of videos and reading a few books, we think we know the answers to all sorts of things that we don't know. The moment you think you know, you're stuck. Stay with "I don't know". This is the beginner's mind. And to develop the beginner's mind is really the fastest way to higher consciousness because then the universe can pour through us. We're not caught in thinking we know.

~

S: How did you decide which belief systems to adopt when you were letting go of belief systems that didn't serve you?

V: Well, I first started undoing belief systems when I was 19 when I realised I'd been programmed or brainwashed by my parents, my religion, my school, my peers and my government. I recognised that I'd been fed a lot of belief systems that weren't my experience, and when I really looked at them closely, there was no evidence to support them. They were just common belief systems, and so I started undoing them. It came to a point that I realised that every belief system is limiting because every belief system has the possibility of creating contraction in us, and really, openness counts for everything. In removing belief systems, we remain open, open, open, open, and this is the right ground for higher consciousness and the right ground for healing the wounds of the Heart and the right ground for Enlightenment. So all belief systems were examined. All of them were examined to a level where doubt was put into them so they lost their power. A belief system that has doubt in it loses its power. If you're into freedom, go with "I don't know".

S: Do we need to be able to intellectually identify our belief systems to remove them or if we open every time that we contract will they eventually remove themselves?

V: Nothing removes itself without intervention. Human beings pretty much are programmed with everything they've got by the age of nine. And those programs become default patterns which run automatically and unconsciously. Unless there is intervention to undo those programs or to change those programs, they don't change. Just by actually letting something go doesn't change it. You actually have to actively undo it to change it, and then you have to practise something different for long enough so whatever you're doing that is different becomes your default pattern.

Human beings are simply programmed and most human beings don't change much after the age of 21. They're pretty much the same until they die unless there's been some form of intervention. The best intervention you can get, of course, is to learn acceptance of life because then life becomes very, very beautiful. When we don't accept life as it is, when we're resisting life because we think it's wrong, or we think it should be done different in some way, we just create suffering in ourselves. When we look at openness, openness requires us to accept life as it is, and this sets us up for higher consciousness and it sets us up for Enlightenment. Openness counts for everything.

~

S: Are morals a belief system?

V: Heck, yeah. And morality, for most people in a lot of ways, is required, but if you can find your Heart, if you can find love, you don't need morality because you will take care of everybody and everything anyway. When you find love, your mind is affected by love in such a way that you just want to take care of everybody and you will do no harm. You will take care of everything and everyone. Morality is required for people who don't have Heart. They need a set of rules to live by because their mind is not tempered by the beauty of Heart. The most beautiful way to live is the Way of the Heart, but that's up to you. That also requires a great deal of openness. Heart tends to appear in openness and disappear in closeness. And so, the more defended and closed you are, the less Heart you are likely to experience. The more open and undefended you are, the more vulnerable you are, the more likely you are to feel Heart, and as you feel Heart, you will do no harm.

S: Can morality help you to find Heart?

V: The only thing that I found effective in finding Heart was openness. Ideas just of the mind don't necessarily work. What works is openness and nothing else. You can try to intellectually understand Heart, but that's not Heart, that's understanding, that's still a mind trip. True Heart is absolutely beautiful. It's the true jewel of consciousness, and if you find Heart and you live the Way of the Heart, you are living the noble path because you will take care of everything and everyone. There is no selfishness in the Way of the Heart. Selfishness is the mind without Heart. For the mind with love, selfishness disappears.

~

S: Why were your worldly pursuits in the way of Heart?
V: Well, I went to a school that taught me how to win and then I went on to study business and become an entrepreneur. Once again, how to win. In a lot of ways, business is the art of war, and the art of war is not about openness. It's more or less about cleverness and closedness. I saw my pursuits in business as in the way of my Heart because I'd become too warlike, and it was really nice for me to let it all go and pursue my Heart. But I don't think that's a requirement for everybody. That's just what I did because I felt that Heart, love, was more important than success in business, more important than making money, because Heart is actually very beautiful.

~

S: I get resentments and I'm aware of them, but can't let go. Any advice for letting go of a resentment?
V: If you're holding on through resentment, you're holding on to resentment. What you're suggesting is that you have no choice and I disagree. You do have a choice. You're holding on to it. You're the only one who can let it go. Let go of the story and stop being a victim of whatever you're thinking about. Let go, let go, let go, or continue to hold on. You actually have a choice here. You choose.

~

S: How do I come out of self-created and useless imaginary thoughts?

V: Put your awareness on what is real. As you're walking, put your awareness on your footfalls, put your awareness on your arms moving, put your awareness on your breath as it comes out and goes back in. Put your awareness on the sounds around you. Put your awareness on the feel of the air around you, the heat of the sun around you. Put your awareness on anything that is real. It will take you out of the dream and back into reality. This is called meditation.

~

S: I've heard you speak about "loose" and "disciplined" minds. Why is a discipline mind important for waking up?

V: When we look at what is the disciplined mind, it's just a mind that can basically behave, really, and stay still. Not carry on all over the place, not go into highly emotional states all of the time, dramatic states all of the time. A disciplined mind stays even, that's all. It's been trained to stay even. An undisciplined mind runs around like a monkey, just here, there and everywhere. They call that "monkey mind" sometimes. A mind that has been trained or disciplined stays even, even when under attack, just as even, and that will support higher consciousness and will support Enlightenment. Anytime that our mind contracts and goes into drama, we're actually going down into lower consciousness, we're going into a dream state. A mind that can stay even, stays with what is real. A mind that can do that is a mind that has higher consciousness.

~

S: Is witnessing the mind the same as analysing the mind?
V: No. Analysing the mind is just another dream you take yourself into and you think that somehow that's doing you some good. Witnessing the mind is very different. You just watch the mind like you're watching someone else's mind. You just watch it, and in the watching you get to see what it's up to. So instead of analysing, you're watching, and then the mind shows itself to you. This is how you can raise your consciousness levels. Analysing doesn't raise your consciousness levels because it's just taking you into another dream. Analysis itself is a dream. Witness the mind and you'll see what it's up to.

You'll see all sorts of things and you'll go, "Well, I don't want to do that, I don't want to do this, I will continue to do this, I will continue to do that", because you're seeing it without judgement. You can then decide what you're going to let run and what you're not going to let run. In analysing, you're just lost in another dream, and a lot of seekers get caught in that trap. They just think that analysing and understanding is going to raise their consciousness levels. No, that's the booby prize. Watch the mind. Witness it without judgement. That's what works.

~

S: Do you have to relive suppressed childhood emotions to get rid of limiting beliefs or can the belief go without reliving the emotion?
V: So, when we say reliving, we're talking about feeling repressed emotions. My understanding and my

experience with healing wounds of the Heart is that what has been repressed needs to be felt so it can be released. It is in the feeling or the willingness to feel that we heal. We don't heal by understanding how we got wounded. We heal by being willing to feel what is there and by refusing to top it up by being a victim. Quite often, if we are wounded, there's a story about us being a victim of someone or something or even ourselves. We can feel that wound until the cows come home and not heal it if we're still topping it up by remaining a victim to whatever circumstance occurred.

So there's two things in healing the wounds of the heart that are important. One is to not keep topping it up by running any form of victim story about it and the second is the willingness to feel it. If we're willing to feel wounding, we can heal it, but most people prefer not to feel. They prefer to try to understand how it all happened and somehow think that the knowledge will heal them. No amount of knowledge ever healed a wound ever. You have to be willing to feel it and that's uncomfortable because wounding isn't just painful, it also has helplessness and hopelessness in it. Two things which we really don't like to feel.

If you're willing to feel those things, you can start to heal what's there. It's up to you. It takes a little courage, the willingness to be with what is, to be tenderly okay, to tenderly welcome what is. And whatever you do, stop the stories that created it in the first place. Something may have happened to you a long time ago. You're the one compounding it now by repeating the story over and over in your own mind. Stop it. Don't be a victim. Don't be a victim ever. Be free of that. Do not volunteer to be a victim. Life is just the way it is.

~

S: I find I slowly contract over time when I'm left to my own devices. This is accelerated when with others who are not interested in awakening. How important is a loving support group?

V: I've got to say that I didn't actually have a loving support group so it's not absolutely required. I decided to start healing my wounds when I was quite young because I recognised that other people could control me through them and I just wasn't into it. We get frightened of feeling abandonment and we get frightened of feeling rejected. We get frightened of feeling all sorts of things. Frightened of the feeling of being shamed, being seen as stupid, and quite often there's wounding attached in there somewhere from our past. And so, we're so frightened to feel that wounding. We comply. We sell out on ourselves. And I just wasn't interested in doing that.

I started looking for my wounding when I was quite young, in my late teenage years, so I could start to heal it. It took a while for me to work out ways to heal wounding. I got involved with a lot of inner child work, even before inner child work was even being published. I started to find a way to be with those children inside of myself or those parts inside of myself that were quite young, that were holding pain, and allowing myself to go in there and actually be with them and release it through the willingness to feel it. I didn't have the support group that a lot of people would have, though I did get involved with a lot of people who were teaching how to heal, were teaching ways that worked, and that did help.

So you can get involved with a group of people who can support you in healing or you can do it by yourself. I think it's probably harder to do it by yourself than it is if you've got a support group. I have created an environment here in Perth where people are in a group and they do support each other in this awakening process, part of which of course is healing the wounds of the Heart. There is a lot of support here – probably the support I would have liked when I was a seeker. It's up to you. You're the one who has to feel your wounds. You're the one who has to do the healing. No matter how supportive someone is, they can't do it for you. You're still the one who has to do it.

I saw the different people who were activating my wounding as teachers. They were showing me where I was wounded and I allowed myself to feel what was being touched and heal what was being touched. Instead of going into rebellion against these people who were triggering my wounding, I was seeing them as my teachers who were showing me where my wounding was so I could show up in there and start to heal it, and that was very helpful.

~

S: Is it best that I have a partner who is also into higher consciousness to support my chances of waking up?

V: You have a partner in life because you love people. That's best. It's lovely to love someone. It's lovely to be loved by someone. It's lovely to share the journey with someone. And you can share it, to a certain degree. It's very difficult to be with someone who's not into Truth if you're into Truth because they're going in a different direction than you, but it's possible. Everybody and everything can be your teacher if you allow it to be so. Every disagreement or every different direction or every misunderstanding can be used to practise acceptance, can be used to practise let-go, can be used to practise openness, the things that facilitate higher consciousness. Once again, it's up to you. How are you going to live your life? Sometimes a spiritual life isn't noticed because you're not wearing robes and you're not wearing beads, but you are practising mindfulness, you are practising meditation, nobody needs to know you are practising self-inquiry. Nobody needs to know. You are allowing yourself to feel your wounding and heal it. Nobody needs to know. All of these things can be done without the world knowing. It's up to you. Only you can do that. Nobody can do it for you.

~

S: Is finding Heart an essential requirement for waking up?

V: No, not at all. Finding Heart will either happen or it won't happen. The awakening of the Heart will happen or it won't happen. My experience is it happens in openness. It happens in unconditional surrender to what is, but someone can actually go directly to

Beingness through self-inquiry and know themselves as Truth directly. This is the fast way. Once awakening occurs, there's probably enough openness to support Heart. You have to see. But you can go directly to Enlightenment without awakening in the Heart.

~

S: Any tips for finding awakened individuals in my area to hang out with?

V: There'll be people talking negatively about them and there'll be people talking positively about them because people who are awake stir everyone up, so some people will love them and some people will not love them. Often you'll hear the negatives and that sets you on alarm. Ah! There's something there. Someone's stirring things up. Because awake people always stir things up.

~

S: Even if I do everything that is required to wake up, will I wake up?

V: No *laughing* There's no guarantee whatsoever that you'll wake up even if you do everything that is required. You can prepare the mind and have higher consciousness. You can find the Heart and love, but Enlightenment is by grace. It either happens or it does not happen. And that side of it, I would have to put down to karma.

S: Can I wake up without an enlightened teacher?

V: Heck yeah. I don't think it's impossible at all to wake up without an enlightened teacher. My understanding through my memory is that we have had many, many, many lives on this planet. And that a lot of seekers have been here before doing this many, many times before and have done a great deal of work to raise their consciousness in previous lifetimes and created enough merit through their good deeds to give them good karma in past lives. So, some people come into this life awake. Some people will sit on a park bench and wake up. But I believe it's all a result of work done previously. And so, if you haven't done the work previously, you need to do it in this lifetime. Some people come in to this life very conscious. Some people come in awake. But my understanding is that's the result of previous work.

~

S: Do I have to be able to rest in no-mind to wake up?
V: Not necessarily. Self-inquiry can take you directly to awakening. Awareness can become aware of itself simply through self-inquiry. It's just that a mind that is actually able to be quiet is more likely to support what is found, that is all.

~

S: A lot of teachers say to me, "you already are that" but that is not my experience. What am I missing?
V: Nothing, you just don't see what's there. You already are that, that's true. Everybody is Beingness. You already are at your final destination. You can't go anywhere to find you because you're already there as pure awareness. It's just that the pure awareness that you are is not aware of itself, so the attempt from the seeker is to use the mind to help awareness turn back to itself so it becomes aware of itself. You are already that. There's no doubt about that. We are all

Beingness. There's nowhere to go. There's nothing to really get. Just turn awareness back to itself.

~

S: If you could give only one teaching on what is required to wake up, what would that one teaching be?
V: Practise openness. Openness counts for everything. If you practise openness, you'll find your Heart. If you continue to practise openness, the ego will disappear because the ego itself is closed. The obstacles will be removed. That that's aware of the mind can easily become aware of itself then. I advocate the practice of openness. It counts for everything.

~

S: I feel guided by Osho. Do you experience his presence and guidance?
V: I don't experience any separation whatsoever from Osho as I don't experience any separation from you. Find yourself as Truth and then you know yourself as one: everything and nothing. The whole idea of separation is ego-based, not reality-based. We are one. Osho is here. There is no separation.

~

S: They have measured brain waves. Is it possible that a Buddha field is a certain brain wave frequency and that neural beats of the same frequency could help?
V: Possibly. I don't know the answer, but it's possibly true. It's just that the instruments that we have which are run with electricity, which is a very gross energy form, cannot produce something as fine as a Buddha field. I believe that love is also a frequency, but our instruments are too blunt, too gross, using

too heavy an energy field in themselves to detect the fineness of love or the fineness of a Buddha field. Maybe it will be possible one day when we become more refined with our electronic equipment. The human mind can detect love because it radiates. The human mind can detect a Buddha field because it's a radiation, because it's fine enough to do so, but the instruments that we have today can't really detect it and they can't produce it, as far as I know, but it would be really nice if they could. Then we could have Buddha fields all over the place and love fields everywhere. That would be an awesome invention.

~

S: Hello, what a blessing. I'm so excited to meet you. It's powerful.

I was guided to you from Kevin Reese, Dr Kevin Reese, and I listened to your podcast with him and then I was guided to Osho and I just feel a powerful presence, his presence.

V: Yes, you can feel what is here. Awareness became aware of itself here 22 years ago. There is a Buddha field here and those who can feel it can feel it, and those who can't can't. This is the same presence that I fell in love with, that I found with Osho. I fell in love with his words as well. He was a very articulate, beautiful man to listen to, but the energy field is the same. He used to describe it as when you go to the ocean, it is salty, when you go to any ocean, it is salty, it is the same. The Buddha field is always the same, and the more surrendered the mind is, the more powerful the Buddha field is because awareness is more on itself than out here. Often when you talk to people who are awake, they're very, very gone because awareness is very, very in on itself. So when I met Osho, he was at the latter stages of Enlightenment, the sattvic stage of Enlightenment where he was so gone. I remember watching videos of him in his younger years where he is more rajasic or more in the world. But as time goes by, the pull in, awareness pulling in onto itself, is stronger and stronger and stronger so there's a heading towards a more silent and more still, a more sattvic way of being in the world. And so after 22 years, the field here has got quite strong.

S: Beautiful, yes, very powerful. Gravity's been pulled together now. Reminding each other.

V: Yes, that's right. And it's a doorway for you into your own self because you're really experiencing your own self to some degree. The Buddha field is just you externally in a way. It's a doorway into who you are. It starts to expand your mind. It starts to quieten your mind and then it's easier for you to have clarity and it's easier for you to self-inquire and discover that space that's behind the mind, that is simply aware, for yourself.

S: I totally lost my mind this week. I let it go. Thank you.

V: My pleasure. My teacher Osho said if you find the light, don't hide it, shine it, and the idea is to find more lights so there can be more light in the world.

S: Yes, we're lighting up this world.

V: Yes.
S: Thank you. I hope to meet you someday.
V: We've just met.
S: In person.
V: Very welcome.
S: I don't tend to travel because I believe that the people who are here need me if they start waking up and need me if they start going into the dark night of the soul, which happens to seekers, and I don't see the point of me being out of the country while they're going through that. So you'd have to come to Australia.
S: Okay. Yeah.

~

S: Does everything in the universe produce the love frequency?
V: I don't know the answer to that question. I know that I see love everywhere and perceive love everywhere, but love is a mystery to me. I perceive it, but trying to understand love, I haven't been able to wrap my mind around it. It just is, and sometimes it isn't. If I'm out here, there's pretty much love for everything. If I go in, there's just vast nothingness. Vast, vast emptiness. So love is a mystery to me. I've experienced it as every particle in the universe and then I've experienced it as something that moves and comes out and touches. I've experienced it as just beauty. But it's still a mystery to me.

~

S: Can you say anything more about the experience of love?

V: Not really. Not really. It's just beautiful. It's worth going for. But it requires our openness. Some people experience love to some degree, but they limit themselves because of their closedness, their defensiveness. If you really want to experience more love in your life, allow yourself to be vulnerable. Allow yourself to be more yin than yang. Allow the world to pass through you instead of letting it bounce off you. Love is the most beautiful thing that we as human beings can really experience and it affects our minds in such a way that we just want to take care of everyone and everything. So love is the true jewel of consciousness, but from my perspective it is such a mystery. It's just here. And it's real. What's thought about it is not real, but it in itself is real.

Enough for today. Thank you for satsang. Good to see you bravehearts here today.

CHAPTER EIGHT

From Darkness to Light

S: Hello Vishrant, can you please talk about the topic "from darkness to light"?

V: It's a metaphor. The darkness is basically dream, and in that dream, people believe that they are a someone who has been somewhere and is going to go somewhere, and it's just a dream. You take away your imagination and the dream doesn't exist. We all know that imagination is not real so the dream that people have of themselves – their past, their future, their analysing – this is the darkness. The light is awareness, consciousness, Beingness, whatever you want to call it. It is our true nature and it is always here. It is just covered from perception by dream, and so the journey – if you like to call it a journey, which is not true either – from darkness to light is simply leaving the dream, turning awareness onto itself so consciousness knows itself.

This is the light, because this is the Truth of who and what we really are. The dream, which is imagined by the mind, is not who we are, but most human beings are identified with the dream, with their mind, with their body. In a way it could be said that they are locked in darkness because that's where their awareness is focused. Spiritual awakening, Enlightenment, is knowing self as Beingness, pure awareness, pure consciousness. This is light, in comparison. And so, the seeker comes from the darkness, comes from dream, and is looking for the light, the light of Enlightenment. By turning that that is aware of the mind back onto itself, that light is revealed. At the same time, it is clearly revealed that the dream and the identity of the "I" is not real, so it cannot be believed to be self.

This process is difficult in a lot of ways because the mind with its dream is basically a survival mechanism, and as such it defends itself. In its constant contracting to the world, resistance to the world, awareness stays locked onto it. Even the attempt to turn awareness back to itself can be thwarted by a mind that is contracting against the world because then awareness goes back to the mind. Therefore, the work for the seeker is an undoing process, undoing the mind, undoing all of the things that create resistance and contraction and that attract awareness.

In Buddhism, we talk about developing an equanimous mind. That is a mind that will stay level no matter what is happening – and this is absolutely possible. We look at our mind, we witness our mind, and we undo everything that causes contraction. We undo the belief systems, we take down the defence systems and we walk through the world in a vulnerable way. But this is not natural and this is the problem. It is natural for us to be contracted and live in resistance to some degree. This is natural. This is survival. Those who have gone beyond that have gone against nature and won, and this is why Enlightenment is relatively rare. The survival mechanism that calls itself "I" needs to learn surrender which is against survival. There's the trap. There's the problem. You're going against the default program of survival by practising acceptance, surrender, let-go, and it's difficult.

It takes a fair bit of work to develop higher consciousness. Lower consciousness is constantly in resistance to the world, contracting and going into story. Higher consciousness, we're talking consciousness of the mind right now, doesn't contract, doesn't go into resistance, stays cool. From this level of consciousness of the mind it is possible to turn awareness back onto itself and for awareness to stay on itself. If it stays on itself continuously, this is Enlightenment. From darkness to light.

Are there any questions, any statements or any challenges to this teaching today?

S: How can people who live in darkness start to find or see the light?

V: For me, I had to go and live in America with an awakened master, Osho Rajneesh, because the dream seemed so real. It was very hard to not believe that I was a somebody who had been somewhere, who was going somewhere and that analysed things. It wasn't until I sat in the presence of an awakened man and found myself disappearing completely as an "I", and there was just space, that I realised, hey, I can't be an "I" because I'm here, but the "I" is not. So for me, it was the presence of an enlightened master who I'd tracked down and gone to live with in Rajneeshpuram in Oregon, America in 1984, and that was the beginning in a lot of ways of my spiritual life. I had started it before that, but it wasn't until then that it really got going, when I recognised clearly that I was not the mind and that this "I" was a fraud.

~

S: Would you say that living in the mind is just darkness, or is there a purer, lighter version of mind?

V: Okay, so I'm sure that people would like to hear that there's a lighter version of mind, but all dream, all thinking – if we're going to use the metaphor of light and darkness – it is darkness because it's not real. Beingness or pure awareness or consciousness is real. The dream thoughts are not real: awareness being light, dreaming being darkness. There is no light in dream. It is darkness because it's dream. Mindfulness training, meditation gets you present to reality out here, takes you out of the dream, helps you to recover from the dream that you're lost in and then gives you an understanding. "Well, I can be here without the thoughts and so if I can be here without the thoughts, what am I really? What's here?"

~

S: Buddha said thoughts become objects. What was he referring to?

V: My take on that is that he was given the understanding that people believe their thoughts to be real as objects are real. The ability to discern the difference between what is real and what is not takes a fair bit of practice because most humans have lived in dream for so long. They believe that what they think is real. That is actually an object. My understanding is very clear: no thought is real, there is no object. What is real is pure awareness, pure consciousness, and that cannot be described, but the closest is probably just vast nothingness itself. That's not an adequate description either.

~

S: Are all objects darkness and only Beingness is light?
V: Ah, so true. So true. We dream the world. We dream the world into existence. What is aware of the dream is of interest to the seeker.

~

S: The Buddha's last teaching was supposedly, "Be a light unto yourself". How does one do this? And can others help or is it a solo journey?
V: So the phrase, "Be a light unto yourself" would indicate that you're trying to light yourself up. That's very early-stage stuff. How about just be a light if you can? If you can facilitate Enlightenment in the vehicle, you as Beingness become a light for everybody that you come in contact with. Like a lighthouse, constantly radiating light, no personal distinction whatsoever there, just radiating the light, the Buddha field. This is the light. Be a light. Wake up. Be a light so others may see.

~

S: So you're saying to become a light so that others can see? Was this your motivation for Enlightenment?
V: It was one of the motivations that was there because 10 years before awakening occurred, I had taken the Bodhisattva vows, and in the Bodhisattva

vows, you become a light so others can see. There is no such thing as selfish Enlightenment. That's actually not a possibility. You can't get enlightened for you because you are not real in the first place and selfishness disappears completely. Even the wanting to become awake disappears completely before awakening. Everything disappears. You are left with absolutely nothing. No past, no future, nothing. This is reality. Everything else is dream. So the mind drops, and in that dropping, which is a surrender, unconditional surrender, Enlightenment is possible. Then awareness becomes aware of itself and a Buddha field is produced by that which is referred to as the light. It allows people to have clarity. It allows their minds to expand and become silent so they can see clearly.
~

S: If time is a mental construct, is space also a mental construct?

V: Take away your thoughts and answer the question. Time is definitely a mental construct. There's only now. Shut your eyes. What space? Without any thought, without imagination, what space? There is just here and now. Now: awareness on awareness, vast, vast nothingness, and out here love, so much love. But this cannot be described by words. It cannot be. It has to be known, and so the endeavour is to turn that that is aware of the mind back to itself so awareness becomes aware of itself or consciousness becomes aware of itself. Then there is a knowing, from the minds perspective of what it all is, but that knowing can't be described because it's infinite.

We just don't have reference points to describe it. Everything we describe from an ego-based reality has reference points so we can understand what we're describing. There are no reference points in Beingness because it is everything. It is a totality. It is omnificent. Yet sages for thousands of years have attempted to try to describe it, but they can't. You have to find out for yourself through your investigation.

~

S: I find myself chasing those glimpses of light I have sometimes experienced. Is that my mind chasing it? Is my chasing getting in the way of being light?

V: No, no, unless the mind facilitates it, unless the mind seeks it, it won't find it because if the mind's left to its own way, its own nature, it'll just keep dreaming on until the body dies. The seeker seeks Truth as self, and it is that thirst for Truth that facilitates the possibility of Enlightenment. Without that thirst, we would not strive to find. We would not remove the obstacles in the way. If there is one desire that is worth having, it is desire to know self as Truth.

~

S: If I turn the world into existence, when do others and I experience suffering? Am I creating the suffering that exists within and around me? And when I realise I am suffering....

V: I'm sorry, but I'll only answer one question at a time. I'm quite prepared to answer any question, but I'm not prepared to be bombarded by questions. Just one question at a time please.

S: Okay, I'll ask the first question. Am I creating the suffering that exists within and around me?

V: Totally. You are totally 100 per cent responsible for your suffering because every human being suffers pain, experiences pain, that's a better way of putting it, experiences pain. We only suffer when we resist that pain or that discomfort. It is our resistance that creates the suffering, not the pain. And that needs to be clearly understood. Pain is just pain. Suffering occurs – whether it's emotional or physical – suffering occurs when we go into resistance to that pain. It is our resistance which we are responsible for that creates suffering. And so, we are 100 per cent responsible for our suffering because we supply the resistance and we have a choice, we don't have to do that. We can start accepting life as it is. We can start accepting pain as it is. We can be willing to be with it without resistance. It's a choice.

~

S: When I realise that I am suffering, why is it so challenging to end that suffering?

V: You're programmed to resist. You've been programmed to contract against pain. You've been programmed to. You are taught by your parents, you are taught by nature – because in nature, our nature is to avoid pain and chase pleasure. We're talking about programming, how we've been programmed. We're programmed to resist and because of this we suffer, but because we're intelligent beings we can learn not to resist, we can learn to accept life as it is, but that's going to be up to you. No one at all can do it for you.

As your consciousness levels rise, you see that your resistance is caused by you, not by what's happening out there. Then you can choose not to resist, you can choose to accept life as it is. Suffering ends. Pain doesn't end because having a human body and being in the world there is pain. But suffering ceases to exist because you are no longer resisting life.

~

S: Could an enlightened person do good by creating a cure for COVID-19?

V: Oh, wow! Enlightenment is just awareness aware of itself. After awakening, you might be lucky that you can even talk, let alone do anything. People project a great deal on to people who are awake that is not there. Anyone, anyone on the planet can wake up. Anyone! Awareness can become aware of itself and stay aware of itself. That person may have no skill in communication so they'll probably be mona (teacher), mona meaning silent. They'll still be radiating Beingness because that's what happens. When awareness is on awareness or consciousness is on consciousness, a Buddha field is produced. As far as doing anything else in the world, who knows? Depending on what skills you had before awakening, they may be used, if anything at all.

I remember when Enlightenment started to occur, I just sat still for six months – 18 hours a day practically doing nothing, staring into space, profoundly content with everything, no motivation to do anything. You see, one of the things that occurs is your mind gets to see the perfection upon perfection upon perfection of everything as it is. The only motivator that I could find to move out and to do anything with people was love. All other motivators had dropped, and because love was present, how that affected this mind was it wanted to help people. It wanted to see if it could help people out of suffering, help people become more conscious, help people become enlightened. There wasn't anything else to do. And even with that, it was nice to sit still and do nothing. So this idea of going out and saving the world? The world is how it's meant to be. There's no mistakes. It's perfection upon perfection upon perfection. I think the only way that you're going to understand is for you to wake up. Our resistance to what is, thinking things are right or wrong, is what creates unrest, a restless state inside ourselves which in a way forbids Enlightenment anyway because it attracts attention to itself.

The acceptance of life as it is is the best. You don't have to agree with what's going on, but acceptance is a requirement. If you're interested in raising your consciousness levels, if you're interested in Enlightenment, that doesn't make you necessarily ineffective in the world. You can operate from acceptance, particularly if love is perceived. Love will have you be in service to everybody until you die because that's how love affects the mind. It just loves to take care of people. Surrender unconditionally and find out for yourself.

~

S: How do you know when to pause before answering or when to answer straight away?

V: I don't. I don't think. I wait for answers. You ask a question, the answer is either there, or it is not there. If it is not there, I wait for the answer. I don't think about it. It's a very different way of being in the world. We were trained at school to rationalise, to use our minds to work things out. But the truth is, we don't actually need to do that at a certain stage because we've been in the world long enough to have developed enough patterns to survive quite sweetly without too much rationalising. So for the last 30 years or more, I've been waiting for answers. A problem presents itself or a question presents itself, so rather than rationalise, I just wait for the answer to appear and it appears because my mind prefers to be silent rather than analysing the thinking. The answer is there or it is not there. Sometimes it takes a second. Sometimes it takes a minute. Sometimes it doesn't come at all, but I'm not concerned. Either it's there or it's not there. Either way, it's okay.

~

S: The next question has been written by Keerti. For a few years, I've been able to go to stillness with little or no effort. However, mind still entertains itself. It seems hopeless. Is it?

V: I don't like hope. It's a dream about later. What I know works is self-inquiry and not touching the mind. The mind comes, you don't touch it. You don't entertain it. You develop a habit of not entertaining the mind because you currently have a habit of entertaining the mind. To change a habit, we need to introduce a new habit, a new pattern. I'm never going to suggest to people that this is easy. But my practices towards the end were simple: self-inquiry and don't touch the mind. And basically I got this from reading the Ribhu Gita: to abide as self and not touch the mind. So you find the silence. Find the stillness. You find that space. The mind presents itself, don't touch it. This is a very high teaching. But it's up to you as to whether you want to follow it or not. I have absolutely no interest in what the mind does or says. The mind here loves silence and it loves stillness. It is pristine.

One of my teachers, a man called Vartman, used to tell a story about not touching the mind. He said, you're walking along in a park, and you tread in some dog poo and it gets on your shoe and it smells. And you don't want to do that again so you wipe it off, and from then on, you avoid treading in the dog poo. You make sure that you don't tread in it. He referred to the mind the same way, as thoughts the same way. It's like dog poo. Once you've trodden in it, it stinks. You don't want to do it again. I enjoyed that. I enjoyed that little story he told. And so self-inquiry and don't touch the mind. Let it go. Stop entertaining it. Don't feed it.

~

S: Hello Vishrant. My question is, what is the way to live life?
V: Okay. How's India today?
S: Yeah, it's beautiful, and nowadays winter just started so yeah, it's good. There is only one problem is just coronavirus, that's all.

V: Yeah, yeah. There's only one way that I know that makes life worth living. I mean, you can live life in many ways, but there's only one way that I know that makes life worth living and that is the Way of the Heart because that is beautiful. For that to occur for a human being, they have to be open because it is only really in openness and undefendedness that we perceive love. When we perceive love, it affects our mind in a way that we want to serve others, serve the planet, serve the animals, serve everything, because this is how love affects the mind. This is the Way of the Heart and this is worthy of giving our attention to. It's worthy of service. My mind chose to serve Heart for 10 years before awakening and in that service of Heart, people were served, my partners, my children, my extended family, my friends, strangers, clients and people who didn't like me. It didn't make any difference. Love doesn't have conditions on it. This is the Beauty Way. This is a way that is worth living. I hope that helps.

S: Yeah, thank you, Vishrant. But can we add self-inquiry and meditation or do we just have to live the Way of the Heart?

V: The way to higher consciousness is like a bird and the Way of the Heart is one wing. The other way is the wing of discipline: self-inquiry, meditation and mindfulness. They're the two wings to make the bird fly in the marketplace. The Way of the Heart is one wing, discipline is the other wing. You see?

S: Thank you, Vishrant.

V: Fly high, fly high.

S: Thank you sir. Thank you.

S: Can you explain how you accepted or surrendered to primal survival mechanisms like tall heights and do you not feel that fear anymore?

V: I had vertigo up until awakening. Vertigo is an unreasonable fear of heights. I discovered it when I was a boy because I used to like to dive off the top of a swimming pool tower that was 30 feet off the pool. Every time I'd go up the ladder, to go up these 30 feet, my limbs would turn to jelly, but I would go up and dive and up and dive over and over again because I was trying to defeat the fear. I never achieved defeating that fear.

Vertigo remained with me my whole life until I was 45 years old. The worst event, I think was in Hong Kong, going up in a lift that was made of glass on the outside of a building and the floor was glass as well. I just turned to jelly, like rubber. I went up in it, but it wasn't pleasant. And then when I had just turned 45, awakening occurred.

I was down in Denmark, a town 400kms south of Perth where I live, and I'd been in a retreat with a spiritual teacher called Vartman. Before the retreat, I'd gone on this walk which was called the Tree-Top Walk where you do this walk above the trees. It was 30-to-40 feet, sometimes 50 feet, 60 feet off the ground, and it was this suspended open mesh metal path that you walked along with hand rails. As I walked along it, I trembled the whole way because I just turned to jelly. After awakening, someone invited me to go and walk on it again to have a chat with them. I walked on it and all fear of all kinds had left. There wasn't any fear left at all. There hasn't been any fear experienced since then. It is gone. It died with the survival mechanism, when unconditional surrender happened.

~

S: If the world is perfect, what is the purpose of COVID-19?

V: What is the purpose of any virus? What is the purpose of any bacteria? They're just trying to live like you are.

Look, I've studied this for so long. What is the purpose of life? I still come up with "to live". There is no other purpose. Life itself. We might look at bacteria and viruses as the enemy, but they're just trying to live too. They're just consciousness in a different form, trying to live as well. Everything is consciousness. All is one.

The purpose of COVID? It's just a virus that is trying to live and it's devastating I think 2 to 3 per cent of the people that it gets into. It's killing them. Not to mention the damage it does to other people who get it. But interestingly enough, have a look at what the human population is doing to the earth. Isn't it something similar to what the virus is doing? But I think we're wiping out way more than 2 to 3 per cent. The only thing that's going to save this planet is higher consciousness yet not that many people are going for higher consciousness. And so, the purpose of the coronavirus? Life. The purpose for human beings? Life. The coronavirus is destructive in that human beings die. That's tragic. Human beings destroying our planet's atmosphere and destroying our climate? Tragic. Everything's just trying to live.

~

S: The following question is from a viewer: What is love? How do I know when I'm experiencing real love?

V: Good question. In my experience, I didn't experience true love until I was 33 years old. I thought I did. I thought the caring I had for my partners, for my family, the kindness, the generosity that I had, I thought that was love. I also thought my attachment to them was love and my bonding, chemical bonding to them was love. So I had all of these ideas about what love was and I thought that I knew what love was because I had felt all of these things.

Then I was lost at sea, 60 miles off the coast in a boat that had sunk, lost in the water for 18 hours with a friend, my girlfriend. We were being circled by sharks, and as I looked over to her and felt the regret of not checking the weather properly before we went out and realising that she was going to die, as I was, something happened and something opened in me and it was love. It was the most beautiful, unconditional thing that I'd ever, ever felt. It was non-directional. It was just there.

It was at that point that I realised love was worth more than anything else I had. At that time, I was a successful businessman, but this little bit of unconditional love that I was experiencing was the true jewel of consciousness and worth going for. Up until that point, I'd lived myself, lived my life as a businessman basically, being successful in the material world, thinking that it was all about owning Rolls Royces and properties and businesses, having a certain image and having the right woman by your side for your looks. It wasn't until I experienced that unconditional love in the water, suffering from hypothermia from being in the water for 18 hours, that I realised I'd wasted 33 years of my life pursuing the wrong thing.

It was nine months later in that year that I walked into my companies and gave them to my staff so I could go on the road and pursue my Heart because there was a clear recognition that I had become a war machine as a businessman and that my business was now in the way of what I knew was truly valuable: the Heart. I don't know the answer to your question. Whether you perceive love or you don't perceive love, I do know this: that the perception of love occurs in openness, not closure; not defendedness, but openness. The more open we can be, the more perception of love we can have. The thing about being wide open is there's very, very little of you in the picture at that stage so the obstacles are not there. Openness counts for everything and it's up to you. You're the one who closes yourself. You're the one who resists life. You're the one who's defended. It's up to you to undo you so you can perceive the beauty of unconditional love.

~

S: Is it true that when true love is found, you shine like a lamp on everything around you?

V: Yes. Yes, it's true. But there's no you doing the shining. There's an absence of you. It is true there is a light, a love light. It's true, but that's because the obstacle has been removed. The thing that contracts, the thing that dreams is gone. There's an absence of you as an "I". You are still here, but without the "I", and then there is just love.

~

S: As I go deeper into my meditation, I can see a lot of beauty and light in the silence and stillness, and also a lot of evil and darkness. Do these two originate from the same source?

V: Probably not. Mind you, everything originates from Beingness, but if we go into the idea of evil more precisely, and we take away selfishness, there is no such thing as evil. Evil exists because of selfishness. As we move through the world, as we become less selfish and more selfless, evil disappears inside of us.

Unfortunately, we live in a world that is quite selfish in a lot of ways. Capitalism is a very selfish pursuit and we live in a capitalistic country. Selfishness is promoted through our newspapers, through our television media, through Facebook. People taking advantage of our self-obsession, making us unhappy so they can sell us products to make us look better. In the name of taking care of self, we hurt other people because if we're selfless we don't do that.

The Way of the Heart really happens as a result of a lack of "I". In other words, no selfishness. This is a beautiful way to live, but you've got to decide to serve Heart. You can't just think, "Ooh, I'd like the Way of the Heart". That would be a nice way to live. No, you actually have to consciously decide to serve Heart and then do whatever it takes to serve Heart. Part of that is letting go of selfishness, letting go of what would cause evil on the planet. The self-obsession. The little lie: let it go, let it go, and be free.

So it comes back to you. See, we look at different things. Selfishness comes from the mind. If we look at light, it comes from awareness being aware of itself, so they're kind of two different things, but ultimately, they're not because everything comes from Beingness or the great Tao. Everything comes from the great mother. It's up to you. Have a look and see. Investigate for yourself. Anything I say is second hand and borrowed knowledge – not worth keeping unless you have investigated and found it to be your own direct experience, and then it's worthy. Never ever believe anyone. Never ever believe. Put beliefs in the "maybe" column. Check it out for yourself. Find out for yourself. Know for yourself through your own direct experience what is true and what is not true. This is the way of the seeker.

~

S: Did you fight the darkness that you found within yourself?

V: Fight the darkness? Heck no. Why would I do that? That's me hurting me. You see, the darkness, or what we want to call darkness, is just part of the psyche. You don't fight it. You accept it, but you don't run it. We all have the good, the bad and the ugly inside of us. We all have that inside of us. You don't fight it. You accept it. You just don't let it run because it might hurt someone. We all have a killer, we all have a thief. We all have a liar, a cheat. We have everything inside of us. The whole world is inside of us. Why go against it? Why fight it? That's ridiculous. That's part of your mind fighting another part of your mind. How can you ever be relaxed when you're doing that? No, you have to warmly welcome all parts of the psyche, but there are certain parts you don't let run. You're not going to let the killer run, you're not going to let the thief run, the liar run, the cheat run, you're not going to. You don't do that, but you acknowledge them and you hold them in tenderness as well so they are accepted – every part of you is accepted. And in this self-acceptance, the mind can relax. When we don't accept ourselves fully, the mind cannot relax. It's not possible because it's at war with itself. Never fight your own mind. Never ever fight your own mind. Accept it as it is. That's best.

~

S: I experience your energy field as light. Sometimes people have described seeing light, seeing light in the Buddha field. Why does this feeling or seeing of light occur and how to facilitate it more?

V: Facilitate seeing it or facilitate creating it? Look, when awareness is on awareness there is a Buddha field and some people perceive it as light. Some people perceive it as just an expansion of mind. Some people experience it as silence. Some people experience it as beauty. Some people experience it as love. Some people don't experience it at all. You want to facilitate it? Surrender your life to Truth. Surrender unconditionally to Truth and give Truth your life. That works.

~

S: There is a saying that goes, "We are all broken. That's how the light gets in." Is this true in your experience?

V: That's a Cohen lyric. It's a really beautiful idea. The light gets in through the cracks where you're broken. Leonard Cohen, I think, wrote and sung a song about it. It's very beautiful. I really liked the song. Ah no, it's not true. It's just an idea. The light gets in. What he's saying about the light, he's really talking about insight: you get to see it all and as a result of seeing it all, there's a potential of changing it all. In witnessing the mind, we see it all. We see what we're up to. We see the liar, we see the good, the bad, the ugly. We see the manipulations, the defence systems, the belief systems – we see it all, and because it's seen, this is the light. This is the reference to the light. Because it's seen, then something can be done about it. It can be altered. It can be surrendered. We don't need to let it run. We don't need to react. We can respond instead because it's seen. I think it's a little romantic to say that the light gets in through the cracks in the brokenness of humanity. I think that's just a romantic understanding. You want to see yourself? You develop a silent witness that watches the mind independently. And then as you start to see, that allows the light in, the insight in, because you're watching from outside the dream.

You're not locked in the dream anymore. The mind is just dreaming away and you have a pattern that is watching the mind. There's detachment there. That works. I wouldn't rely too much on brokenness allowing the light in, though I do love Leonard Cohen. I really enjoy his songs.

~

S: I've heard you say that an awakened teacher is like a flash of lightning that lights the path. What is the best thing for a seeker to do in the presence of a teacher who carries the light?

~

V: Look at the path. Look at what's being pointed towards. Don't look at the teacher. Look at the path. Look at what's been pointed towards. See what needs to be done while the light is there.

There's a story about two men being lost in the jungle and they can't get out. It's a dark night. It's wet, it's windy, it's raining, and lightning strikes. One man looks at the lightning and says, "Oh, how wonderful that is! So bright! Look at the sky." The other man looks at the path and sees the way out. Always be the man that looks at the path to see the way out. Forget about the lightning. People get caught up in looking at the teacher, admiring the teacher, admiring the one the light's coming from, and they miss where the teacher is pointing.

S: Where are you pointing?

V: I'm pointing at you, dude. Pointing back at you. You've got to look inside of yourself. You've got to turn awareness back inside of yourself. You can't find it outside of you. You are the light. You just have to find it inside of you. Self-inquiry, asking the question "What's aware?" might help. Undoing all of the defence systems that keep you contracting to life and all the belief systems that keep contracting you to life, that'll help, but it's inside of you. I'm pointing at you. You are already at your final destination. You are Beingness itself. Discover that. Turn awareness back to itself.

Thank you for satsang. Good to see you bravehearts here today.

CHAPTER NINE

Going with the Flow

V: Welcome to satsang.
S: Hello Vishrant, can you please talk about the topic, "Going with the flow"?
V: If someone's going with the flow, they're in acceptance of life as it is. They're not resisting. They're not contracting. They're not defending. They're in flow, and this is a very beautiful way to live, to live in flow. The opposite of it is contraction and resistance which is just suffering.

So if we're looking at developing a life that is equanimous, we've got to look at what takes us out of flow.

What puts us into resistance? What is the obstacle to flow? A mind that is supporting flow is a mind that is relaxed, and a relaxed mind supports higher consciousness. A relaxed mind is the right kind of mind to develop. If we just look at what makes us happy and we see, well, if we're in resistance, we're not happy, if we're contracting, we're not happy, if we're defending, we're not happy, when are we actually happy? And if we really examine it, we'll find that we're happy when we're in flow, when we're not resisting, when we're in a state of let-go.

So if you're really interested in raising your consciousness levels, you practise acceptance and let-go. You practise moving towards a continuous flow in life rather than an up-and-down mixture of flow and contraction. Life becomes very beautiful when we let go. When we stop trying to resistantly control our environment it becomes very, very sweet, but only you can do that. Most people have not been programmed to do that. Most people have been programmed just to resist, contract, defend, survive and suffer, and really, we don't need to. If we're willing to let go and go into flow, life is beautiful.

You're responsible for how you think. You're responsible for your mind and you can create a situation of flow. Nobody else can do it for you because the world is hard for everybody. There are plenty of things that you can resist. There are plenty of things you can contract to. There are plenty of things that will make you feel like defending yourself, but only you can keep you open. Nobody else can do that for you. You're responsible for the way you think and so training the mind to let go, training the mind to accept life as it is, is something that you do for you. It makes your life better. You watch people who are suffering. You watch them closely and you'll see that they're in resistance. You'll see everybody has troubles and that some people don't resist, they are just okay with it. They don't suffer.

From my perspective, suffering is a choice. But there is a funny thing in that. You actually have to be conscious of that choice. You have to be conscious enough to see that you don't need to resist life, that you can accept life, that you can let go and still be effective as a human being in the world. Practise and see. The only thing that's going to change default patterns is practice. Practise and see.

Any questions, any statements, any challenges to this teaching today?

S: Does going with the flow mean allowing my mind to do whatever it wants?

V: Heck, no. If the mind does whatever it wants, it's going to start resisting life, start contracting, start defending itself, because that's what it's been programmed to do. You've got to teach it not to do that by letting go and by accepting. This is a discipline that you apply to the mind to teach it a new default pattern, a new way of living in the world. If you don't teach the mind to let go, if you don't teach it to accept life, well, nothing's going to change the mind itself. If you watch it, if you just witness it, you'll see how it creates suffering for you, and in that witnessing, you don't want to be involved anymore. So just start looking at the mind watching it, seeing what it's really doing rather than believing whatever story it's telling itself. Just witness it and you'll see.

~

S: It seems to me that most people aren't interested in hearing that suffering is a choice. Why would this be the case?

V: Most people think it's not a choice. They actually think that they do suffer and that it's at the hands of something else besides themselves. Mind you, you're the only one who can supply resistance to what is. Something bad can happen, something negative can happen, but you're the one who can accept it or resist it. Therefore, it's your choice. You make a decision. If you become conscious enough, you choose not to resist and you choose to accept life as it is. That does not make you an ineffective human being, it just means that everything you do will be from a place of openness rather than a place of closure.

S: So what would going with the flow look like in a person?
V: What it wouldn't look like is probably a better way to put it. It wouldn't look like they were suffering. It wouldn't look that way. It would actually look like they were cool, calm and relaxed. It would look like they were happy. Suffering doesn't look that way.

S: How do you stay in flow once you notice all of the suffering that occurs in the world, like the poverty, murders, wars and greed?
V: Well, it's a choice whether you contract against those things or you don't. This has always been the case in the world. The world has always had tragedy in it. It's always had poverty, and it's just how it is. Now, you can contract against that or you can stay open. It doesn't mean that you don't have empathy and compassion for those who are suffering. It just means that you're open and you're not in resistance. It means you're still in flow. We don't have to close. We can remain open.

S: It seems that some people use going with the flow as an excuse for not taking any action in their lives.

How is this different from really going with the flow as you're talking about it?

V: You don't have to take action in your life if you don't want to. That's your choice. I don't see it that way. I see that you can actually go with the flow and make a difference on the planet. You can be in acceptance of life and still put up a protest if you need to, but from a place of acceptance and openness. The moment we close, there is a chance we might get angry and that's a form of violence. We don't need to go there. We can actually change things without being angry. We can change things from openness. We can change things from a place of acceptance, or do nothing, but that's your own choice, it doesn't matter. What really matters is whether you're raising your consciousness levels. The problem with not accepting life as it is, the problem with resisting life, is when we get involved in resistance, we take ourselves into lower consciousness. This whole game here is about higher consciousness, not about lower consciousness. And it's up to you. How are you supporting higher consciousness? Or are you supporting lower consciousness? And of course, the question, what do you really want?

~

S: Sometimes to make things happen, it feels like I become forceful, pushing against the current. How can I get things done in a state of flow?

V: By relaxing inside, and the only way we can truly be relaxed inside is if we're in acceptance of what is. The moment we move to non-acceptance of anything, we are no longer relaxed. Life's the way it is. It's neither good nor bad, it really just is the way it is. We can judge it as good or we can judge it as bad and get caught in the story or not. Getting caught in the story isn't going to change anything. If you want to change something, you do something, you do something about it. But you can do something about it from a place of openness. We don't actually have to be closed. We don't have to be lost. We can be wide open and make a difference. Up to you.

~

S: After meditating, or after satsang sometimes, I have no motivation to do anything because I'm so peaceful. Is it possible for me to find this motivation to do things without using force and resistance?

V: People ask these questions. Life is so cool if you just let go. So you find all of this peace after satsang or after meditating? Sure, because you're actually quietening the mind, you're teaching it how to relax. Why don't you just continue to teach it how to relax? Why do you have to stop? Why do you have to go back to resistant patterns and lose the beauty that you find in meditation, the beauty that you find in satsang? Because only you can create a disruption. Really, the world is just the way the world is. Your reaction to the world is what creates the problem. Learn to relax your mind. Learn to be cool. And we learn to be cool by the practice of acceptance and let go. What do you practise? Because whatever you practise, you're going to be good at.

~

S: You were talking about supporting higher or lower consciousness. I tend to be result-orientated and I find this takes me into lower consciousness. Do I have to remove this result-orientation or is there another way to be more conscious?

V: Result-orientation is a dream of the future. It's not real, and as long as we have our awareness on a dream, we're not very conscious at all. We may be conscious of the dream, but we're not conscious of reality. We're actually dreaming. And so, there's nothing wrong with having goals in life, but actually being goal-orientated, where you're constantly thinking about the goal, that's just another dream. It's not a reality, and of course, it's a dream that involves a certain level of suffering because there will be the hope that the goal is achieved. On the other side of that there'll be the fear that it won't so you're living in a bit of a nightmare-type dream. It's best just to be present to what is, to be here now, with what's real. There's nothing real about what you think. You want to go into flow? Well you don't go into flow dreaming, you go into flow when you're out of dreaming, when you're just here, in reality, in nature, without resistance, when you're natural. Practise that.

~

S: When I'm able to find silence and stillness, I feel really peaceful. But the moment that things don't go my way, I lose that peace. How do I keep my awareness on the silence and stillness when things are going wrong?

V: There's only one way: it's if you have practised acceptance. There is no other way. If you're not practising acceptance, of course, you're going to lose it. Which comes back to what are you practised at? It's that simple. What are you practised at? No amount of intellectual understanding will help you. You can know all of this stuff to your marrow. It won't help you. What changes our default patterns is practice. If you're practised at being open, if you're practised at being accepting, if you're practised at let-go, you will be good at it, even when you're under stress. But if you are not practised at that, why would you be good at it? It doesn't work that way. It works because you practise it. You want to be in flow, practise being in flow. And of course, the best time to practise is when we are under fire, when things aren't going our way. That's when we can practise acceptance. That's when we can practise let-go. So don't see the world as negative. See it as opportunities to practise something that can bring you peace.

~

S: Patel's talk about following the path of least resistance, is that something that you consciously practised?

V: Once upon a time, until it became my habit. You see, if we practise meditation long enough, we'll become very present by default nature. If we practise mindfulness often enough, we'll become present to reality because we've practised it. If we practise openness enough, it becomes our default nature. Whatever we practise is going to be our default nature, so I'm open – yeah, there's no doubt about that – all of the time, but not because I'm doing anything.

It's just a default pattern that's been trained into me through practice. I cannot see any point in resisting life because I'm just not into my own suffering.

~

S: Sometimes you say that tolerating is still resisting. How do I switch from tolerating a situation to warmly welcoming it?

V: Of course tolerating is resisting. It's waiting for it to be different. You're in dream, you're not even present to reality. You're dreaming, you're tolerating, you're waiting for something to change rather than being with what is. You're dreaming, and in that dream, you're resisting, you're tolerating. Of course it's resistance, and it's a nasty dream. How long do you tolerate before it becomes intolerable rather than just accepting it as it is?

~

S: It seems that in being human, there is an ever-flowing stream of emotional ups and downs which may appear to be chaotic at times. What does one need to do to not get caught in emotionality?

V: Emotions are just part of the human psyche. They allow us to let things go. Crying is the great healer. But if you're really interested in not getting caught, remember that emotions are still part of the mind, the same as thoughts, so develop a silent witness that just watches. Then you find yourself detached from everything. It's like you're watching someone else's mind, and because you're watching, you don't get caught in it, so a lot of emotionality actually disappears because you're not caught in the mind. You're not caught in the stories anymore. You really want to get free? Develop a silent witness that simply watches the mind.

~

S: I know that you were a martial artist. The Shaolin monks practise martial arts. Do you think martial arts helps the seeker towards going with the flow into higher consciousness?

V: Look, any discipline that involves surrender, that involves acceptance, that involves non-resistance, is great for raising consciousness levels. In martial arts, I learned how to die because if you go into a bout, if you go into full-contact training with the fear of death, you've already handicapped yourself. You have to go in in a space of let-go so you can be there 100 per cent. And so martial arts trained me to let go, trained me to let go of dying, trained me to let go of being hurt, because if I entertained those thoughts, I would handicap myself in the game. First of all, those thoughts are dreams. They're not real, which means if I entertain them, I'm not even present to what's going on. Martial arts really are a discipline that can enable you to learn let-go, can enable you to learn acceptance and surrender, and I definitely used it for that.

~

S: So in regards to learning how to die, are there ways of learning how to die without putting myself in physical danger?

V: Well that would be best, wouldn't it? Because you put yourself in physical danger, you might die. But you've got to understand what meditation is. Meditation is simply being aware of what is real all of the time. Now, what is not real is your mind's story, your mind's thoughts. They're not real. And so, if you're in formal meditation and you're watching the breath and a thought comes in and you abandon it and come back to the breath, you're actually practising dying. You're practising dying to the thoughts. But that's going to be up to you. What do you practise? You see, I fell in love with meditation. I fell in love with present-moment awareness because it's real. There's nothing real about what you think, and because we've all been programmed to be problem solvers, that's where most people live: in their heads solving problems. To me, that's just ... that's a nightmare. What about just being present to reality? Just being here? That's really, really nice, but it takes practice again because we went to school, a lot of us for 12 years, and then some people went on to further education at universities and colleges and we learnt to live in our heads so we could solve problems so we could get a certificate on the wall saying we could do such and such. Unfortunately, most people never recover from the dream that they've been put in. They end up problem solving until they die. The practice of meditation is really the practice of reclaiming reality from the dream that you're lost in. Up to you.

~

S: Does the practise of self-inquiry, when I get caught, help with learning let go and being in flow?
V: Does "the practise of self-inquiry when I get caught" help? Why would you be practising self-inquiry when you're caught? I'm sorry, but that question

doesn't make a great deal of sense to me. It sounds like you're using the practise of self-inquiry to avoid things. That's not the go. Self-inquiry is to turn awareness onto itself to discover your true nature. It's not to be used to avoid life. The same as meditation. Getting present to reality is not a way of avoiding real life. Even if it's being used for that, it's being used incorrectly.

~

S: To meditate properly, I feel that I need the perfect conditions. Is that because I'm not practised enough? Or am I practising the wrong way?
V: Right now is always the perfect condition to be present to reality. Right now is always the right time to be present to reality. This is the perfect condition to be present to reality: right here, right now.

~

S: I noticed there is a lot of peace in letting go, but why do I forget that so often?
V: Yeah, people get insights and then they forget because they're dreaming and the dream seems so real and so important that you forget other things. Most people who are dreaming don't realise they're even dreaming. They just think this is ordinary, this is normal. Well, it probably is for them, but when you get present and you stay present, dreaming becomes abhorrent. Because it's not real. This present moment is very beautiful. Things are very beautiful. It's a bit like being a little kid again, in wonderment because you're here and you're enjoying the here and you're enjoying the now. You're not locked in some dream about wanting something later or regretting some-

thing from before. You're here. You're in this moment. It's up to you. It's really up to you. You're the one who's going to either meditate and practise mindfulness and get back to reality or continue dreaming. Nobody's going to help you. It's totally up to you.

~

S: I prefer being in nature or in a quiet hall to meditate. When you say right now is the perfect condition, what do you mean?

V: Meditation needs to be every moment. Meditation simply means being aware of what is real. The only thing that is not real is what you think. Meditation is being here all of the time. And when you were a little kid, up to probably about the age of four or five, you were pretty much present every moment. And then you went to school and you learnt how to live in your head. It's very beautiful to be present every moment. It's lovely. And if we're looking at Enlightenment, Being, awareness aware of itself, well that's being present to reality. Something can appear in it, but present to reality is beautiful. What do you want? Do you want higher consciousness? Or do you want lower consciousness? Keep dreaming: lower consciousness. You go to higher consciousness, you start moving more into the moment, more into reality, away from the dream, because the dream is lower consciousness and everything you think is dream.

~

S: I understand that meditation is to be present every moment. But do you think it is useful to take some time out to do formal meditations or go on meditation retreats?

V: If you haven't, if you're a dreamer, yes. If you're not practised at being present, yes. If you're practised at being present, well you're practised at being present. It's like asking the question "Should I stop banging my head against the wall?" Yes, you should. Of course, meditate, do formal sessions, go on retreats, do whatever it takes to reclaim reality from the dream that you're in. Whatever works. Be pragmatic. Up to you.

~

S: In practising mindfulness, I've started to notice that everything comes and goes. Can this observation help me learn to be more in flow and become more content?

V: Not really. The only thing that helps you be in flow is acceptance and let-go. Understanding doesn't really help. You'd think it would, but it doesn't. Because basically, if we have to understand, it means we have to contract and then let go. If we're truly in flow, we're not letting go, we've already let go. Practise acceptance. Practise let-go. That works. You can listen to me about let-go. You can listen to me convince you to let-go, but that won't help unless you practise.

~

S: So with flow, does there need to be an internal welcoming to all experiences?

V: Well, we look at: how do we accept life? How do we actually practise acceptance? And from my perspective, it is an openness to what is and openness to whatever's appearing rather than a closure or a resistance. And so yeah, we need to practise, need to continue to practise, but you can warmly welcome, that works, but that's also a practice, isn't it? Whatever appears you make okay. You don't resist anything. This is way to live. This is the way to live beautifully.

~

S: Is going with the flow the same as being in touch with your intuition?

V: Not really. Being in touch with your intuition you could still be closed, you could still be in resistance to some degree. I don't think they match up that well. Being in flow just means that you're open no matter what is happening. It's a way of life. It's a way of living. As a matter of fact, it's the Way of the Heart. Because when we're in flow, when we're open, when we're not resisting life, when we are present to reality, Heart becomes very prevalent. The beauty of Heart becomes very prevalent in that openness, in that non-resistance state. The openness that's created by an acceptance of life and let-go creates the right environment for people to perceive love. Very beautiful.

~

S: Can a person be in a state of flow and still be in masculine or in yang energy?

V: Not really. When we look at different energies, yang energy is outgoing and tends to be resistant. Yin energy is more of that receptive type of energy, and that facilitates flow way better because there's no resistance in it. If we really want to be in flow, we need to embrace the feminine, we need to embrace yin, and in embracing yin, we're also embracing the Way of the Heart. It's very beautiful, very lovely to do so, but it's against our survival mechanism. It's against our nature to do so. We're programmed to survive, we're programmed to resist, we're programmed to contract, we're programmed to defend. Somebody who has got to a level where they're not resisting life and they're in a state of flow has done a great deal of work on themselves to remove the obstacles that are in the way, and more than likely, you'll find that these people are happy to a large degree because they're not creating suffering for themselves.

~

S: I noticed that young kids are usually naturally in a state of flow. Why do we lose this as we become adults?

V: I don't know if that's actually true about young kids being in a state of flow all of the time because they go into resistance. They get defended. They're learning how to be adults. Someone who's in a state of flow all of the time is someone who's actually really practised at it – someone who's practised at acceptance, someone who's practised at let-go. Little kids don't really practise that. They're just not aware of everything yet. They're not programmed badly enough yet.

You try being present to reality for a while, try meditating and being present to reality for a while, and then see what contracts you. And anything that contracts you will probably have a belief system attached to it. Remove the belief system and be free. I find that most belief systems are prisons.

And that brings us back to the subject of true rebellion. When you start challenging your own belief systems, you're rebelling against your own mind. This is the true rebellion. Not against the world. It's not against a government or a policy. It's against your own mind, because that's where suffering begins and ends. You create it by your resistance to life. By rebelling against your mind and removing the belief systems that create contraction in you, you're disempowering them. You are winning. Because if you contract and you create suffering in yourself, you have lost. You've been defeated by your own mind. Rebel. Examine your mind. Stop believing it. Examine it.

~

S: I've heard it said that if you just go with the flow, everything will work itself out. Do you think this is true?

V: I don't know. Go with the flow and find out. When you say "work out", of course everything works out, whether it works out the way you want or not. That's another story. I don't know the answer to that question.

~

S: I've heard some teachers say that everything is a part of and an expression of flow or divine intelligence. Do you agree with this?

V: I really don't know. See, people want to know because they want to be able to control. They want to understand so they can control their environment. I really don't know. I don't have this need to control my environment. It's all okay. I don't need to know. I'm absolutely okay with not knowing. That way I can stay present to reality. Not knowing, in wonderment, it's quite nice. Have a look at why you need to know. What is this all about? Why do you need to know? The only thing that you really need to know is that surrender is the answer and if you practise it, you get good at it. You don't need to know anything else. But people want to know this, they want to know that. They want to be able to control everything because they don't like the chaos that we live in. But the truth is everything is chaos. We don't really know what's going to happen next. We might be able to guess or we don't know. We don't know when we're going to die. We don't know when we're going to get sick. We don't know when we're going to have accidents. We don't know when our family is going to suffer. We don't know. There are so many things we don't know, but we try to know, we try to control everything. It's okay. Chaos is actually okay.

If you can be okay with chaos, you can be relaxed. And the world is chaotic. Your controlling it is creating tension in you.

~

S: The Taoist teaching of instead of moving against life, letting life move through you, sounds lovely, but I find it very difficult to do. How do I get to this point of letting life move through me?

V: Well, the moment you stop resisting, then life just moves through you. Life moves through you anyway. But most people don't experience that. They experience their resistance because it shows up. Life is . . .

life is a flow: birth-life-death. Chaos. It's all a flow. The moment you resist, you're kind of in your mind, stepping into a stuck place. But really it just keeps flowing anyway. It's not like you can stop it. The chaos continues and if you can be okay with that, you can be rested inside yourself.

~

S: Can openness and going with the flow make us vulnerable to manipulation by others whose motives may not be good?
V: Possibly, yeah. You can be wide open with people. Doesn't necessarily mean you're gullible or naive. You can be open, you can be accepting, you can be loving. You don't have to be ripped off because you're being gullible, you can still say no from openness. This idea that people think "Well, if I accept, I've given up" – no, you've just accepted. You're practising openness now. Of course, there are dishonest people in the world, it's the world we live in. So what! You don't have to be ripped off by them. Being vulnerable is very beautiful. Doesn't mean you have to be ripped off. As a matter of fact, being vulnerable is the Way of the Heart. It's up to you.

~

S: I think I have an unconscious assumption that responding to stressful situations with stress is an appropriate and productive response, the opposite of flow. How do I change this habit?
V: Well, the same way we change any habit: you do something different than what you've been doing. We developed our habits through practice. That's

how we developed them, by doing them over and over and over again until they became default patterns. If we want to reverse a habit or change a habit, we have to do something different than that habit for long enough until there's a new habit. So it's up to you. Whatever you practise, you will be good at. You want to be free? Practise openness.

~

S: Does being in flow also mean treating others kindly, being caring and generous?

V: Look, if you practise openness, you'll find your Heart, and when you find your Heart, you will be kind and you will be loving and you will be caring because that's how the Heart affects the mind. That's how love affects the mind. You want to be those things? You can be fraudulent in those things. You can just do it from the mind. Without Heart. But when you do it from Heart, it's genuine. You just want to take care of people. You just want to be kind to people. You just want to be generous. This is the beauty of Heart. This is the beauty of love. Love is really the true jewel of consciousness. And in flow, we find it. In contraction and defensiveness, we do not. When we're resisting life, there's not much love around – not being perceived at least. You want to receive love, you live vulnerably and open. This is the way.

~

S: The Tao Te Ching says "That which offers no resistance overcomes the hardest substances. That which offers no resistance can enter where there is no space." It sounds like it is referring to being in flow. What is it that offers no resistance?

V: In a state of let-go, everything comes in. When we offer resistance, we're putting up a force that blocks everything. If you want to live in yin, you want to live in vulnerability, you don't offer resistance, you let everything go, you relax your mind. This is a very beautiful way to live because this supports Heart. It supports a beautiful way of living. If all we do is operate from yang, which is that outgoing, powerful energy, life is missing the subtleties, it's missing the beauty. It's missing the softness, the gentleness. It's missing the receptivity.

I love the Tao Te Ching, Lao Tzu's book. I love Taoism. It's very beautiful how it puts the different ways of being in the world. If you're truly interested in the Way of the Heart, which I feel Buddhism is about, embracing the yin is the way. Becoming open, becoming vulnerable is the way. Allowing yourself to perceive more love is the way. And instead of becoming more than, you as an "I" become less than. This is the way to higher consciousness.

~

S: Why and how do you see perfection in everything?
V: In satori, in deep satori, there is nothing but perfection upon perfection upon perfection. Come back out here with your awareness and move to the mind in all its judgments and you see fault. You don't see the perfection because you're looking through the filters of the mind. You're not looking to see that everything is perfect because the filters of the mind

are such that they make it look like it is not. Beyond the mind, pure Beingness, perfection upon perfection upon perfection, is actually reality. There are no mistakes. Everything that happens is meant to happen the way it is, otherwise it would never have happened.

~

S: How can I facilitate love to flow through me?
V: Get rid of you. There's only one thing that blocks people from perceiving love, and that's them. Love is always here, but your closure, your defendedness keeps you from not perceiving it. You want to find love in your life? Open up, be vulnerable, live in the world in a vulnerable open way, accepting what is, and then there's love everywhere because it's always here. If you're not perceiving it, it's probably because you're too closed. That's all. Somehow you've got a defence running, somewhere unconscious or conscious, up to you. You're responsible for you. You're responsible for your openness. You're responsible for your closure. You're responsible for your defendedness. Up to you.

~

S: Is going to university to study environmental science and management in order to stop and reverse destruction of life resisting reality?
V: There's nothing wrong with going to university to study environmental science so you can help this be a better place. There's nothing wrong with that at all. But can you do it from a place of openness or are you going to close up and do it from a place of closure?

That is resistance itself. Because there is enough darkness on this planet already without you going into more resistance. Look at it. We don't need more resistance. We don't need more darkness. We need more light. In openness, we are light. In resistance, we're just more darkness, and there's enough of that on the planet already. Operate from a place of openness and you find Heart and then you take care of the planet from a place of Heart, a place of loving, not a place of disturbance, of resistance, of defendedness, but from a place of love. There's nothing wrong with going to educate yourself in a way that will help the planet. That's brilliant. But can you do it from a place of love rather than a place of anger or a place of business? Can you do it from a place of wide openness, vulnerability and love? Because that's going to have a very different message in it.

S: Are you saying that where we are coming from is always more important than what we are doing externally?

V: Exactly. That's exactly what I'm saying. Two people can do the same thing: one can do it from love, and the other can do it from closure and as a form of internal violence. It's like, the Sea Shepherds out there trying to protect the oceans from all sorts of different things. But are the crew doing it from a place of love of the ocean and love for everybody or are they doing it from a place of closure, defendedness, vengeance? Our attitude is what's going to make the difference. The last thing this planet needs is more violence, and every time we close and go defended, we're preparing ourselves for violence. Practise openness. It supports Heart. And we can do everything from openness. We can change the world if we want from a place of openness, from a place of Heart, from a place of light, because Heart is really true light.

~

S: What do you mean when you talk about bringing the light and the darkness into the world?

V: That's a subject. That's a big subject. Every time we go into dream, we're going into darkness, really, because we're going into dream. It's not real. Every time we go into love, by practising openness, we're going into light because it's a vibration. I call it light, but it's just a vibration. But it's a vibration of beauty. Closedness, resistance, anger – these aren't beautiful. As a matter of fact, anger is violence. We are not going to save the world through violence. The only thing that can save this planet is higher consciousness, and higher consciousness dictates that you be open. Closure keeps you locked in lower consciousness.

Thank you for satsang. Good to see you bravehearts here today.

CHAPTER TEN

Why Taking Offence Doesn't Work

V: Welcome to satsang.
S: Hello Vishrant, can you please talk about why taking offence doesn't work?
V: When someone does something or says something that you don't like, you consider it a possible insult. The moment you take offence, you hurt yourself. They don't hurt you. You hurt you. They've said what they've said or done what they've done. That's the world. You're the one who can either hurt you or not hurt you now because you're the one who's responsible for your reaction. If you take offence, you are hurting you. Now, that might be hard to get, but they're just the world and they're doing what the world does. You're totally 100 per cent responsible for your reaction to anything, and if you take offence, if you really look at it closely, you'll see that you are hurting you. They're not hurting you. You are hurting you because somehow you've turned yourself into a victim. You've volunteered to be a victim of them and you've reacted accordingly. This needs to be seen at a deep level. You create your reaction. You are responsible for it. If you take offence, you hurt you. Nobody hurts you but you.

This is, in a lot of ways, a high level of maturity: taking responsibility that you make yourself feel.

The world doesn't make you feel. Other people don't make you feel. You make you feel. And this is a high level of maturity. What's the point in hurting yourself? What do you gain by taking offence, except suffering for yourself?

Are there any questions, any statements, any challenges to this teaching today?

S: You said in your discourse that this has to be seen at a very deep level. How does this happen?

V: Well, I was very lucky in that when I was 19, I got a copy of a book called The Handbook to Higher Consciousness by Ken Keyes, and in this book, he outlines how we volunteer to be victims. There's no such thing really. It's our reaction to what is that turns us into a victim or not. Bad things can happen and a person can see themselves as a victim of it or not. They can see it and go to blame and start becoming a victim and hurting themselves – or not. It's a choice.

At that time, at the age of 19, I was quite victim-orientated like most other people. People don't like to think they're victim-orientated, but if you're blaming the world for how you feel – for how you are in any way, shape, or form – you're definitely victim-orientated. If you're taking offence, you're victim-orientated, and I could see that I was and I chose not to be anymore. I chose not to be a victim of life. I chose not to volunteer to be a victim, and in so doing, decreased by I don't know how much the amount of suffering that has happened to me over this lifetime because victims' lives don't work and they just create suffering with their resistance to what is and it changes nothing except they suffer. So I was very fortunate in that I got this book The Handbook to Higher Consciousness and studied it back to back, over and over again until I got it, and then practised not being a victim – practised not blaming other people, the world, for my experience; taking full responsibility that I make myself feel, that nobody can do it to me.

~

S: I'm having problems at the moment. I hear what you say and it makes so much sense. I don't read newspapers and stuff like that, but a friend of mine gets me to get the paper and I pass it on, and on Friday, I saw the headline. Apparently Clyde Palmer is intending to sue the Australian Government for $38 billion or something like that, and despite the fact that I know, I understand everything you say, I just lost it. I literally had these thoughts of "If I could get a rifle and get near that bugger, I would murder him". Now, how do I practically get to "it just is" and allow it to be? Could you give us any advice on that?

V: I'm a fatalist. Whatever it is, is, and whatever happens is meant to happen. I don't see mistakes. I don't see errors. I see perfection upon perfection. I see if Clive Palmer does sue Western Australia and does win the 38 billion or whatever, and everyone has to pay $12,000 out of their own pocket to cover it, well, I see that as what's meant to be rather than wrong because I'm seriously not into my own suffering. The moment we see something as wrong, or even right, we're in trouble. That's when our mind starts going off. How do we know in God's big picture for everything that Clive Palmer isn't supposed to sue Western Australia? And when? How do we know? How do we know it's not Western Australia's karma, the people in West Australia's karma to have such a big loss?

S: But just to clarify that when he lost his battle with Western Australia, he's now suing the Australian Government.

V: I know, I'm following it. It's fascinating. This way of talking about karma, think about the karma of Western Australia and the karma of Australia, considering the genocide that white folk inflicted on the Aboriginals here.

S: Yep, I can understand that.

V: You know, there's a lot of negative karma floating around in Australia as a result of the past here.

S: Right. There's one other issue I'm finding really hard to deal with and that's the story of the little girl, the little four-year-old girl who disappeared. It's like, I don't try to get stuck like this, but as you can hear that really affected me. How could that sort of thing be just what is?

V: I don't argue with reality ever. I just accept reality as it is. It's tragic. You know, we look towards nature, and really, the big animals eat the small animals, the old animals, the sick animals. It's what is. There's no such thing as fairness really, that's some mind-made understanding that doesn't exist in nature. And this poor little girl who's been either abducted or wandered off, it's tragic, but you know, this happens around the world all of the time. Little girls and little boys get into terrible situations and because we don't read about them, we don't think about them, but it's happening every day. It's not just that this has happened in Australia. I'm sure this has happened around the world, probably by the hour. We live in a tragic world where everything dies. We live in a tragic world where everything gets to cease, and we can accept that or not accept that. If we don't accept it, we've got a serious problem because we're out of touch with reality. This little girl who's been lost, it is absolutely tragic. It's absolutely tragic, but this is the world we live in and it hasn't just become like this. It's always been like this.

S: Yeah, I totally hear and understand what you say, but can you give me and maybe others some pointers on how to accept it without letting it tear us apart?

V: Okay, so my process is really simple. I just don't think about things. You see, if you weren't thinking about it, you wouldn't be hurting over it, and your thinking about it isn't changing anything. If your thinking about it changed something, if it somehow helped this little girl, well, that would be worthwhile, but you're dwelling on it and running it over and over in your mind. How does that help anyone, including you?

S: Yeah, I get that.

V: I don't live in my head anyway, but I just don't dwell on the negative. I don't see any advantage in doing that to anyone. People who dwell on the negative create so much suffering for themselves and then they share it with everybody else. How does that help anyone? That just brings more darkness onto the planet than is already here.

S: And the irony of it is that I actually hadn't been thinking about it until today's topic started. And then it sort of triggered first the Clive Palmer thing. And when I was talking to you about him, just suddenly out of the blue came this remembrance, and yeah, technically, I can understand.

V: You've got to remember that the news is popular because it's negative. People like hearing negative stories so they rake up these negative stories to present to us. I mean, it's been going on forever and a day, you know that?

Negative news is popular. Positive news? Not so much. Sensationalism is popular and they are definitely sensationalised in the Clive Palmer thing and the little girl thing. I mean, we could go to a country like India and find so much poverty and so much suffering if we wanted to get our cameras there, but they're not interested so they don't go there.

S: Yeah well, you and I have both been to India, and we've experienced that for ourselves and because it's there every day 24/7 it's like it doesn't impact on us so much because there's an acceptance of that's how it is.

V: Yeah, and that's the key. In a lot of ways, the key to not suffer is to accept this is how life is rather than resist it because your resistance doesn't change anything. If it did, it would be worthwhile, but it doesn't.

S: Yeah. I mean, there's an old cynical saying: if it's good news, it's not news. And as a result, I actually gave my TV away to the Salvation Army maybe six or seven years ago, but maybe I should just stop looking at the paper when I just carry it from one place to the other because, as I said, it just really touched me so badly. I don't have to tell you that. You can feel that.

Yeah, I understand what you're saying. I will do my best to just accept that that's the way it is and there is some reason for it happening otherwise it wouldn't be happening.

V: I don't know if there's any reason. I really don't. You know, we try to justify things, but I don't have a justification for a kid, a little girl going missing. I don't have a justification for Clive Palmer. I don't really. I just don't bother dwelling on it because it doesn't change anything.

S: Yeah, that's true, except for our own mental state.

V: That's right. You can take yourself down the chute with these kinds of thoughts and it doesn't help you. It's like when people turn themselves into victims and take offence. It's like, how does that change anything? You know, I get offended by Clive Palmer, you know, suing Australia for 30 billion or whatever. How does that change anything? Just hurts you.

S: Yeah. Thank you. I'll take that on board for the rest of the satsang.

~

S: Hi Vishrant. You said we are responsible for how we feel, nobody else is responsible, and that we can put it on others. I have a tendency to blame myself. And it's... that's victim-orientated thinking too, isn't it?

V: Yeah. You turn yourself into a victim in three ways, really: a victim of someone else, a victim of a situation or a victim of yourself – but they're all victim-orientation, aren't they?

S: Yeah, that's what I wanted to talk to you about. And so sometimes it's like being defeated by my own self. And it's tough.

V: Yeah, look, the best thing you can do is love yourself. Accept yourself as you are, broken maybe, and love yourself, and then it's easy to love the world and accept the world. While you're in non-acceptance of yourself it's hard to accept the world and love the world.

S: Yeah, and then there are situations where people close to me put blame on me. And that's a different situation. And they are being –

V: That's okay. Why not? If they want to blame you, let them blame you. It's none of your business. That's their trip. What other people think of you is none of your business. It's their business.

S: So is that a belief system that no one should blame me that I need, one needs to undo?

V: Heck, yeah. I get blamed for all sorts of things that I don't get involved in. But such is life. It's how it is, you know? People are crazy.

S: Okay. Thank you. Thank you so much.

V: You've just got to love everybody: the good, the bad and the ugly. You've got to love it all. It's best.

~

V: Hello Marcus.

S: Hey Vishrant. I wanted to add on a question about Kalimba's situation. I wanted to know if he doesn't read the paper, knowing what's going on, how's that any different than escaping reality?

V: Sorry? You have to make your question a little bit clearer for me. I'm not sure what you're actually asking. Sorry. Can you try again, Marcus?

S: Yeah. If Kalimba avoids reading the news and avoids the papers, how is that not escaping the reality?

V: We could spend all day watching negative news programs if we want. CNN and Foxtel can help you with that, or not. Choosing not to watch the news constantly isn't really escaping reality. It's just not listening to the propaganda that's being put out that's probably negative. I mean, just in our daily lives, if we're present to what we're doing, we're not escaping reality. Just because we don't want to watch negative programs on television doesn't mean we're escaping reality. We're just making a choice that's probably healthy. I mean, you know, I was involved in the news. I was involved in publishing. It's all about negativity. It's what people want to hear. If you fill yourself up with that it's toxic because it's non-stop, you know? It's non-stop negativity.

S: Right, and I wanted to add on too, I live in a violent neighbourhood so there's also things that go on that's not on the news – that they don't show on the news – and I only hear them from, you know, people in my community. What about, what about that?

V: Yeah well, that's how it is. Violence is all around. Depends where you live. But if you're living inner city, there's quite a lot of violence. It's just what is. It's just what it is. You either accept it or you don't accept it. If you don't accept it, you suffer incredibly.

If you accept it, well, you don't suffer. It really comes down to what you accept or what don't you accept, because you're creating your reality by your non-acceptance or your acceptance. The world is going to do what the world is going to do. If you're living in a rough neighbourhood and there's a lot of violence, that's what is. You can accept it or not accept it. Your choice: suffer or not suffer.

S: Right, also I don't want to add on to it, the violence, so I wanted to ask like, does waking up turn people into pacifists?

V: You come around someone who's awake and you'll find profound peace, because that's the energy field. The Buddha field has profound peace in it, but you know, people can still be violent. It's human nature in a lot of ways to be violent. When we look at our primal animal level of human existence, it's quite ferocious. I mean, we're at the top of the food chain. People go out and kill animals to live.

We live with violence, you know. I go shopping to the supermarket and I pass the butchers. For me, because I'm a vegetarian, it's like walking past the morgue. But that's what is. I don't object to it, it's simply what is. This is the world we live in and I accept that, you know, because I'm not into – I'm really not into – creating suffering for myself. The moment we don't accept something, the moment we go into resistance, the moment we take offence, we are now hurting us. And for what? For what, Marcus, does it change anything?

S: One more question. I wrote, "I have a belief that if I don't have any questions, then I failed as a seeker".

So my question is, to be a successful seeker, do I need to have questions?

V: Okay, you're looking at the guy who always had his hand up in the room when he was with his teachers because I knew that the transmission that occurs between someone who's awake and someone who's a seeker is invaluable. If I couldn't find a question in my own mind, I'd look around the room at all of the other people and the people I knew and I'd know that some of them had questions that they didn't want to ask because they were embarrassed. I would ask those questions.

S: Thank you, Vishrant.

V: It's nice to talk to you, Marcus.

S: It's nice to talk to you too.

~

S: The next question is as follows. Is it okay to avoid people or situations that are doing things to offend us?

V: Heck, yeah. Someone wants to insult you, you don't have to put up with it. You can walk away. If you can't walk away, you put up with it. There's nothing wrong with moving around. In Buddhism, in teaching, if someone's disrespectful to the teacher or the Dharma, the teaching needs to stop because it's been disrespected. There's nothing wrong with stopping. There's nothing wrong with walking away. We don't have to put up with things if we don't want to. We can walk away, but can we accept that that's what is? That's the key. Are we okay with it being that way? Even if we walk away, is it okay? Because if it is, we can find peace. If we go to objection, if we go to take offence, well, we are now hurting ourselves. For what? It's like throwing a tantrum and expecting mummy and daddy to come and pick us up. Doesn't work though, particularly as adults. Mummy and daddy won't come and pick us up.

~

S: Hello Vishrant.
V: Hi Neil.
S: I've had people in the past who would constantly try to offend me, and I tried my best not to react to it even though I was getting offended. I acted as if I'm not offended and tried to avoid them. But I noticed that every time when I was avoiding, it escalated, and they were offending me even more and finally I had to say something or do something to just stop that from happening. Was there a way in which I could have handled the situation differently? I had to react?
V: Well, you could have responded instead of reacted. You could have responded by saying something like, "That really hurt me when you said that" and see where that goes, you see? But you do it from a place of acceptance. You do it from a place of openness. You don't do it from a place of closure. The whole deal is, in a lot of ways, in higher consciousness, to remain open, no matter what is happening. If someone decides to insult you, there's no need to stay. You can walk away if you like, but you can also continue the dialogue, tell them how it makes you feel, or walk away. The only thing that defeats you is when you take offence – and they didn't defeat you, you defeated yourself.

S: Right, and sometimes it's difficult to avoid these people, like a co-worker who is always sitting right next to me.

V: Oh, that's how it is. You know, I operate in this world with a way of acceptance because it's the only way that allows you to remain peaceful. It's the only way also that allows you to serve Heart and stay awake. You operate from acceptance. The moment you start operating from resistance, you are taking you to hell.

S: Right, and I also wanted to know what karma is? Is it something like . . . you do good and good will happen to you, but if you do bad, bad will happen to you? Is that what karma is?

V: Yeah, that's how it works. Whatever you put into life, you get back. This is why Jesus said, "Do unto others as you'd have others do unto you". He was right on board with karma. We get back what we put in.

S: And what if our forefathers did something wrong? Will we get to pay for what our forefathers did?

V: That's a possibility. That's a possibility, yep. If you want to gain good karma, become a nice person, become generous, become honest, become loving, become caring. Become a lovely person. What a lovely way to live.

S: Right. That's it, thank you Vishrant.

V: Hello Abhayi.

S: Hi Vishrant. My question is something like what Neil just asked. There are people who will not understand until I take offence and shout back at them or yell or something like that. In such situations, what can I do?

V: Can you shout from a place of openness or do you have to be totally contracted or even partially contracted to do so? See, I'm not advising people or teaching people to be ineffective in the material world. I'm teaching people to be open in the material world. Can you say no from a place of openness? Can you say "this is enough" from a place of openness? You can if you practise acceptance. You can if you practise openness. In a lot of ways, in raising our consciousness levels, we're opening more and more and more and becoming more and more vulnerable, and in that vulnerability, in that openness, there's more and more love perceived. But this has to be practised because it's not natural for us. It's natural for us to close up, particularly if someone's offending or seems to be offending us. For someone not to close, for someone to stay open, is actually unnatural. It's something we have to learn, and we learn it through practice. It's the only way. If someone upsets you, you can say, "No, that's enough". But can you do it from openness? Or are you going to contract and get angry and say it from that place and do it from that place which is also creating suffering in you? You see the difference, Abhayi?

S: Yeah, I am able to understand that.

V: Well, understanding is the beginning. Now you need to practise it because you're not going to be good at it. Nobody is until you've practised, and then you get good at it.

S: Right. Another thing I noticed is, when I'm open I am relaxed, and people can see that and they tend to be more... I mean, take more leeway, or start giving the same advice, old advice, like dye your hair, or do this thing, do that thing, which I don't want to do. I feel like the more I am open and relaxed, people start taking more advantage.

V: But giving you free advice isn't taking advantage of you Abhayi, it's just giving you free advice. There's a difference between them holding your head over a basin and dyeing your hair. That's different! Them giving you free advice, you can always say "No, I don't want to". And can you say that from a place of openness? Or are you going to close to say it? On the weekend, I was involved in a charity ride called the Pink Ribbon Ride which was to raise funds and awareness for breast cancer, and we had to wear something pink and I had a nice pink windcheater on. But the leader of our group decided that my hair needed to be pink as well. Now, I knew he wanted to do that. He had one of those spray cans, you know, with the pink dye in it, and I kind of stood way back so he couldn't get me, but then when we came to one of the stops, he caught up with me and he had the can in his hand. I could either walk away or run away or go Yes and I just went "Yes". And the beauty of Yes is, it's all over then, except I had pink hair, which I had to wash out later.

Acceptance is so cool. Resistance just causes suffering. Practise acceptance. Okay Abhayi?

S: Yeah. Thank you very much Vishrant. Thank you.

V: Thank you. . . . Hey Tharanga.
S: Hey Vishrant, my question is, so when I get angry or annoyed at somebody, I can kind of just feel that anger building up inside my body and I'm aware of it, but I just can't help but to act out on it. How do we get better at just being okay with it? Like, it seems very difficult.
V: Well, you're producing it through blame. Anger needs blame to survive. If you haven't got blame involved, you haven't got anger because that's the fuel that fires anger up. If you have a look at, well, how am I blaming? Basically, to be angry, you have to be a victim of something. You have to be a victim. You have to have turned yourself into a victim. Blame is how we turn ourselves into victims.

If you really examine anger thoroughly, without blame, it dies. So stop the blame. Accept that people are doing what they're doing rather than objecting to it in an aggressive way, because anger is aggressive. You know, people are going to do things you don't like until you die. It's just the world we live in, but do we really need to get angry about it? Do we really need to close that much and go into such a defensive mode? When someone does something we don't like, it probably creates a touch in us, it hurts somewhere, so we react to that hurt by going to blame which empowers us because anger is empowering and it takes us away from the feeling of the touch, but it's a form of violence. You know when someone's angry with you and expresses it at you, they're injecting you with a toxic energy, because anger is a toxic energy.

It hurts. It's violence. I was very much like that as a teenager and I just decided I didn't want to be like that anymore, so I stopped it. I examined how anger worked. I examined the nuts and bolts of anger and then found ways to not get involved in supporting it because I didn't want to be violent with people and I didn't want to be violent with myself. It's up to you. You're the one creating your reaction. Nobody's doing it to you. You're responsible. What do you think, Tharanga?

S: Yeah, that makes, that makes a lot of sense.

V: It does, doesn't it?

Even if you decide to do what I'm saying, you're gonna fail a lot of times before you succeed a lot of times, but that's how it works. Whatever we practice we get good at. If all we do is practise supporting anger, well, that's all we're ever going to be good at.

S: Yeah.

V: And really, it's not a good thing to support because basically it hurts us and it hurts others if we inflict it on them.

S: I'll keep practising that.

V: Good for you.

S: Thanks, Vishrant.

V: Thank you.

S: The next question has been submitted by Nadia: It seems like my mind is working separately from me. Random words and melodies that don't have anything to do with life situations or people I know are constantly in the background no matter how much I concentrate on doing something or while meditating.

It's like the subconscious belief is that if the mind stops working, I will die, so it repeats random words because there's nothing to think about. I don't get involved in it, because it makes no sense, but it's always there and nothing seems to work with this for more than three seconds. Could you please give me advice?

V: Okay. Okay. It's difficult because your mind's being activated by a lot of different stimuli. A mind that stays equanimous, a mind that stays silent, is a mind that has learnt to surrender and that takes a hell of a lot of practice. It doesn't happen by mistake, because it's against nature. If you can learn to let go more and more, if you can learn to accept life more and more, if you can learn to absolutely be okay with what is, you'll start finding more peace. Your mind's being activated because it's programmed to object. It's programmed to run story. When you were born you didn't run story, you were blank, you were just blank. Then you learned all of these different ways to live in your head. We went to school to learn to live in our heads. Reclaiming reality from living in our heads takes a fair bit of practice because it took a fair bit of practice to put us there. Present moment awareness, meditation practice, enables us to be more present to what is real, but at the same time, we need to learn to let go. We need to learn to be open, we need to learn to practise acceptance so the mind can be at peace with what is, and that's going to be up to you. And I'm never ever going to tell someone it's easy because it's not. It's hard. But what else you got to do? What else is worth doing except raising your consciousness levels which happens as a result of openness, acceptance, surrender – the very things people don't want to do? People just want to be right. Unfortunately, just wanting to be right keeps you in sufferance and usually changes nothing.

S: The following question has been written by Brian: Can you find the Way of the Heart through silence and stillness?

V: Heck, yeah. Openness supports Heart. Now if we're wide, wide open, the mind isn't even moving because every thought in a way is a contraction. The I-thought is a contraction. If we're wide open, Heart is pretty easy to perceive because there's nothing in the way anymore and it's always here. It's not like love is somewhere else. It's always here. In the practise of openness, you start perceiving love for all things because you can perceive it. The obstacles have been removed, the barriers, the defence systems. Openness, from my perspective, counts for everything. It is the Way of the Heart. It is a way towards Enlightenment.

S: The next question has been written by Jeremy: Hi Vish, Jeremy here. I'm interested in knowing more about fear of judgement.

V: First of all, fear is not real, it's a projection, and everyone's going to judge you anyway. It's just how it is because we're programmed to judge. All human beings are programmed to judge. It's how we survive. It's how we get by. We judge things and we make decisions based on those judgments. So for sure, people are going to judge you. For sure. That's what's going to happen. Now, the only way that I know how to be okay with that is to be okay with that. To be okay with the worst. Let people think what they think, that's their business. What are they going to do to you, really? What are they going to do? Are their judgments actually going to really hurt you or are they just judgments? So let them judge. Find a way to be okay with letting them judge. Because if you look at yourself, you judge people. We all judge. Now how harshly we judge depends on how we're made up inside, but everyone judges to some degree. It's how we navigate the world. Make it okay for people to be judgmental. Make it okay for them to get it right. Make it okay for them to get it wrong. Just make it okay and be free, because when we don't make something like that okay, we hurt ourselves, and gosh, why would you want to do that? Be in acceptance of people as they are. Be in acceptance of their judgments. Be free.

S: The next question has been submitted by a viewer: How to overcome the pain of dad's death?

V: Why do you want to overcome it? Why can't you just allow it to be there? Why can't you just make it okay that it's painful? Stop avoiding it, be okay with what's there. It's okay to feel pain. It's okay to feel loss, it's human. It's okay. Make it okay instead of resisting it. Instead of trying to change it, make it okay. Let it be. Make it part of the tapestry of your life. It's not the totality of your life, it's just a small piece of it. Make it okay and be free or go into resistance to it and hurt yourself. This is your choice. It's just part of the tapestry of your life now, this loss. Such is life.

S: The next question has been written by Manisha: How do you resolve past life trauma?

V: Be willing to pay the price. It's very simple. You see, anything negative that happens to me, that's okay. That's just me paying back an old debt. Anything positive happens to me, that's okay. That's just me receiving credit for something I've done. It's all okay. I'm willing to pay my debts. I don't see things as bad or negative really, I just see things as they are, and if it happens to be negative, well, that's just me paying back a debt. And I'm willing to pay back my debts, past life or this life.

S: The next question has been written by Chris: When you sleep at night, do you dream?

V: No, I haven't had a dream for 21 years. I go into the darkness and in the morning, I come out of the darkness. Usually about five hours of darkness. Fully rested.

S: The next part of that question: What function does dream play in an unenlightened mind? Does being lucid in a dream help in any way?

V: My understanding of dreams is quite often they're related to unfinished business that we have during our lives in the daytime and so we dream at nighttime. But I also think that they're related to how we operate during the daytime. Like if you spend a lot of time dreaming during the daytime, why wouldn't you dream at nighttime? And people think you have to be asleep to dream. No, all you've got to do is be imagining something, that's dreaming. A lot of people live in their heads the whole day, dreaming their life away, and then they go to sleep at night and continue the dreaming, quite often dealing with undealt with business. Dreaming just stopped after awakening. It just stopped. It's quite cool.

S: The next question has been written by Bhagwati: As you said not to think negatively, does positive thinking bring about a good change in the person and situations?

V: I don't promote positive thinking because it's just another head trip. It's just another dream and I'm not into teaching people how to dream. All I say is don't support negativity because human beings are naturally buoyant. We don't need positivity to be buoyant. We are naturally buoyant. We're born buoyant. What drags us down is negative thinking or negativity. Just don't support negativity. Don't drown yourself. I don't in any way really support people practising dreaming positivity because I'm not into dream. I'm into reality and I love reality.

S: The following question has been written by Kelly: When meditating, does the length of the breath make a difference?

V: I think what makes a difference when meditating is the amount of time you practise more than anything else. And so if you practise meditation long enough, you get to be very, very present, and this is the object in a lot of ways. Meditation or the practise of meditation allows us to reclaim reality from the constant dream that we're lost in, and when I talk of constant dream, I'm talking about the constant thoughts, because with meditation, you're putting awareness on something that is real, over and over again, until that becomes your habit. And once that becomes your habit, present moment awareness, this is brilliant. That practice is what works and length of time is what works.

S: The next question has been written by a viewer: Is it okay to cut off negative people from one's life? When people find out that I'm trying to better myself by being on the path, they expect me to forgive and forget and still engage but I see it as negativity and I don't want to deal with it over and over again.

V: Okay, look, if you want to raise your consciousness levels, hang out with people who are raising their consciousness levels. It's that simple. The people or the company that we keep affect us quite strongly. You really want to go to the heights? Hang out with people who are going to the heights. It's up to you. The people you hang out with are going to affect you and are going to affect the quality of your life. Choose friends who are going in the same direction. Choose people who are putting Truth as an important part of their life. Choose people who are putting Heart as an important part of their lives. But that's up to you. Whoever you hang out with is going to affect you and you are going to affect them. This is how it is.

S: The next question has been written by Prem Utsaah: Hi Vishrant, when I don't take offence, I then feel like not responding to someone's negative behaviour. It seems like a waste of energy then. How can one remain open and still respond?

V: There's no need to respond if you don't want to respond. Just remain open. If people want to be negative, let them be negative. You want to walk away from it? Walk away from it. Just remain open. That's the key. Remain open. And how do you do that? Practise acceptance because acceptance allows us to remain open.

Acceptance is so beautiful, because it allows us to perceive the Heart, love, the most valuable thing here. Matter of fact, the only valuable thing here, love. You really want to receive love? Practise acceptance. Practise openness. Serve Heart, best of all. What a wonderful world this would be if more people were serving Heart, and it's up to you. Don't wait for other people to do it. You do it. You serve Heart. You open up. This is your journey.

Thank you for satsang. Good to see you bravehearts here today.

About Vishrant

Vishrant is a contemporary mystic who offers a pragmatic path to higher consciousness.

He made a fortune in publishing as a young man, retiring at the age of 28, and then as a world traveller and student of personal development later met controversial Indian guru and spiritual teacher Bhagwan "Osho" Shree Rajneesh who initiated him into the world of higher consciousness and enlightenment.

That encounter led to Vishrant tasting unconditional love during a terrifying shipwreck off the Western Australian coast and then glimpsing his own true nature. After these revelations, he gave his multi-million dollar company to the staff who had served him so diligently for a decade, and then set off around Australia barefoot for the next four years while searching for how to open his Heart once and forever.

After Osho's death in 1999, Vishrant committed himself to the Way of the Heart while working as a naturopath and psychotherapist, running men's encounter groups and later serving a crop of Advaita Vedanta teachers who started visiting Western Australia at the end of the 1990s. Vishrant woke up in 1999 in the presence of one of those teachers.

Since then, Vishrant has held satsang and retreats, and runs a Mystery School in the Perth hills which is also available online for those seeking to find their true nature.

Vishrant's teachings are pragmatic and free of belief systems and religious ideologies. He sees himself as a reality teacher rather than a spiritual teacher and says spirituality has become an overused word. His invitation is for people to investigate the Truth through their own direct experience.

To get involved, visit vishrant.org.

www.ingramcontent.com/pod-product-compliance
Lightning Source LLC
Chambersburg PA
CBHW021057080526
44587CB00010B/277